Piazza Armerina

SS — 1C17

Archaeological Sites

General Editor: Malcolm Todd

Professor of Archaeology
University of Exeter

Already published

Hengistbury Head
Barry Cunliffe

The Walls of Rome
Malcolm Todd

Epidauros
R. A. Tomlinson

Piazza Armerina

R. J. A. Wilson

Louis Claude Purser Lecturer in
Classical Archaeology, Trinity College, Dublin

GRANADA
London Toronto Sydney New York

Granada Publishing Limited
Frogmore, St Albans, Herts AL2 2NF
and
36 Golden Square, London W1R 4AH
515 Madison Avenue, New York, NY 10022, USA
117 York Street, Sydney, NSW 2000, Australia
100 Skyway Avenue, Rexdale, Ontario M9W 3A6, Canada
61 Beach Road, Auckland, New Zealand

Published by Granada Publishing 1983

British Library Cataloguing in Publication Data

Wilson, R. J. A.
    Piazza Armerina. – (Archaeological sites series)
    1. Romans – Sicily   2. Piazza Armerina
    (Sicily) – Antiquities, Roman
    I. Title   II. Series
    937′.12   DG55.S5P/

ISBN 0 246 11396 0

Typeset by A-Line Services, Saffron Walden

Printed in Great Britain by
Mackays of Chatham Ltd

Granada ®
Granada Publishing ®

To Jocelyn Toynbee
with affection and gratitude

Contents

List of Illustrations

Photograph Credits The author and publisher are grateful to the following for permission to reproduce illustrative material:

Alinari: 42, 54, 59; Bromofoto, Milan: 44; K. M. D. Dunbabin: 28; Fototeca Unione, Rome: 5, 11, 13, 14, 15, 18, 43, 46, 58; German Archaeological Institute, Rome: 26, 27, 36; Soprintendenza archeologica, Agrigento: 3; Soprintendenza archeologica, Syracuse: 49.

All other photographs are by the author. Illustrations 8, 12 and 16 are taken from G. V. Gentili, *La villa erculia di Piazza Armerina: i mosaici figurati* (Rome, Istituto poligrafico dello stato, 1959). I am also most grateful to Mrs M. Lyons who drew illustrations 1, 23, 47, 48, 50 and 51.

Preface

The late-Roman villa at Piazza Armerina is the most opulent single country building of that epoch so far known. No fresh general survey on Roman art or architecture fails to come out without a page or two dedicated to it, and in addition the site has engendered an enormous specialized literature. The specialized articles and books have all been in languages other than English, apart from a brief and now out-of-date summary by Sear (1970), and the detailed treatment of the mosaics in K. M. D. Dunbabin's *The Mosaics of Roman North Africa* (1978). The latter appeared after an early draft of this book had been written, but our standpoints differ remarkably little and our very similar conclusions have been reached independently. The aim of the present work is to provide a concise account in English of as many aspects of the villa as possible within the scope allowed by this series, and to explore in particular the status of the villa within late-Roman villa studies as a whole. In this respect two recent discoveries elsewhere in Sicily are of supreme importance, and I am grateful to Dr G. Voza, their excavator, for discussing them with me, and furnishing me with photographs. The book could not have been written without the generous co-operation and assistance of Professor Ernesto de Miro, Superintendent of Antiquities at Agrigento, and of his staff at Piazza Armerina. I was also fortunate in being able to discuss two of the French villas, Montmaurin and Valentine, with their excavator, M. Georges Fouet, on site. Katherine Dunbabin, Charlotte Westbrook and Malcolm Todd, general editor of this series, have kindly read through my manuscript and suggested a number of improvements. So also has Jocelyn Toynbee, but my debt to her is a far greater one. To her stimulating example, to her encouragement and friendly advice unstintingly given over many years, I owe more than words can express.

Trinity College, Dublin, 1.x.80   R.J.A.W.

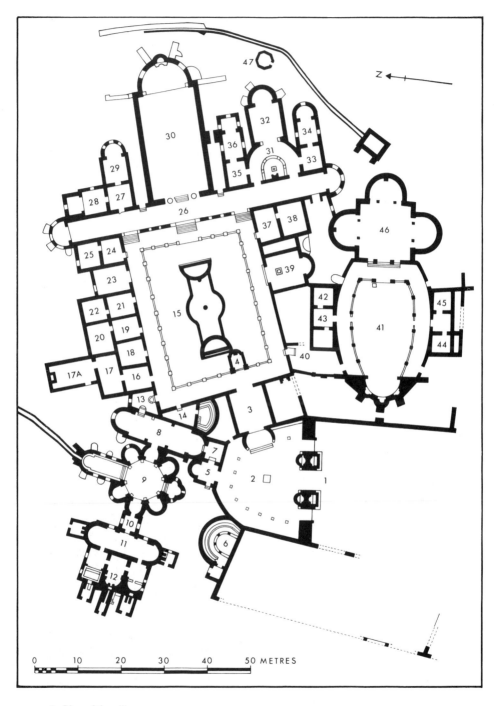

1. Plan of the villa

Chapter One
Layout and Date

The Roman villa which is the subject of this study lies 550 m above sea level in the Casale district of central southern Sicily, 5½ km by road south-west of the modern town of Piazza Armerina. The villa is secluded and does not enjoy an extensive panorama (plate 2). The main group of rooms faces westwards towards the gentle Nociara stream which flows 200 m from the villa, but beyond it rises Monte Navone (754 m), while to the north the site is shut in by Monte Mangone (777 m) and on the east by Monte Saldano (727 m). Only to the south does the ground open out and become less hilly: here stretches an extensive tract of rich, rolling arable land, at the centre of which, 6 km south of the villa, lay the Roman market centre of Philosophiana (see plate 47 for a map of the area).[1] The hills just mentioned belong to the southern end of the Heraean range *(Montes Heraeae)* which in antiquity were covered by oak forests much admired by Diodorus;[2] and today hazel shrubs, pine trees and cypresses, as well as oaks, grow in profusion in the vicinity of the villa.

2. General view of the villa from the west

Discovery

That ancient structures lay at this spot has long been known: parts of the villa still stand up to 8 m high and must always have been visible.[3] Local antiquarians first mention the site in the middle of the eighteenth century, and the earliest recorded investigation, about 1761, discovered 'vestiges of an ancient temple adorned with mosaics and with a flooring of ancient marble'.[4] The destruction of a mosaic is documented in 1804, and the activities of the notorious British consul Robert Fagan, who obtained a permit to dig there four years later, resulted in the sale of two granite columns from the villa to the mother church in Piazza Armerina.[5] Sporadic exploration continued later in the nineteenth century, and part of the mosaic in the three-apsed hall (see number 46 on plate 1, to which all subsequent room numbers refer) was uncovered in 1881, but systematic work on the villa only commenced in 1929 when the indefatigable Paolo Orsi (plate 3), who did pioneering work in all periods of Sicilian archaeology, uncovered more of the same pavement.[6] Giuseppe Cultrera, superintendent of antiquities at Syracuse, continued excavation in 1935, 1938 and 1940–1, exposing the oval court (41), some of the flanking rooms, as well as the south apse of the Great Hunt corridor (26), but further work was interrupted by the Second World

3. Paolo Orsi (left) and Rev. Tranchina during work on the three-apsed hall, 1929

War.[7] The rest of the plan of the villa as we know it today was laid bare by G. V. Gentili in just five rapid campaigns between 1950 and 1954, when the soil was stripped from the ancient structure and the full sumptuousness of the mansion and its decoration was revealed to an astonished world. No other single building in the Roman Empire has yielded such a vast expanse of mosaic flooring – calculated as covering some 3,500 sq. m – and a flood of learned literature poured out in the 1950s and the 1960s on the date and significance of the villa, on the importance of the mosaics and their contribution to our knowledge of late-Roman art, and on possible candidates for ownership of the mansion. Gentili himself contributed to this literature with a number of books and articles,[8] but only his first interim report illustrated any of the small finds;[9] the rest, and any section drawings of archaeological levels, if they were made, remain unpublished. Even the dating of the whole complex was based mainly on stylistic criteria of the floors themselves rather than on any 'hard' archaeological evidence. It was with frustration at this state of affairs that Andrea Carandini sank a few trenches in 1970 in order to reveal more about the chronology of the building,[10] and he and his pupils have set in hand a detailed study of other aspects of the villa left unpublished by Gentili, a study which is still continuing. A programme of conservation, of both walls and mosaics, has also been carried out, first by the Superintendency of Antiquities at Syracuse,[11] and subsequently by that at Agrigento under Professor Ernesto de Miro, in whose care the villa now is. Only a few of the mosaics have been lifted and consolidated. Most of the structure was covered by perspex roofs in the 1960s and catwalks erected on top of the walls to provide adequate viewing facilities for the many thousands of visitors who flock to the site each year, but the mosaics in rooms 4 and 42–5 are still normally covered by sand. More recently, in 1977, a similar roof has been erected over the 'Basilica' (30) to enable its marble floor of *opus sectile* to be permanently exposed.

Layout of the villa

The villa at Piazza Armerina in its present form (plate 1) is substantially the product of a single building plan, with possibly one major and certainly some minor modifications carried out during or shortly after its construction (see below, p. 38). When precisely that was has been the subject of lively debate (below, p. 34), but it now seems reasonably certain that the villa as we see it today was laid out in the first or second decade of the fourth century AD.

The mansion is a single-storeyed building[12] constructed throughout of mortared rubble faced with small irregular pieces of local brown stone. There is no attempt at coursing except at the corners of walls and at

4. Mosaic in the peristyle corridor, animal heads, detail

other points of structural importance, where larger blocks, more carefully laid, were employed. The house is entered through a monumental triple archway (1), ornamented with Ionic columns, niches, and a pair of fountain-basins (plate 57); the latter are mosaic-lined and have a decorative strip of wall mosaic featuring birds and plants. The entrance leads into an irregular D-shaped courtyard (2) with a central fountain-basin and a surrounding portico decorated with a polychrome mosaic of fish-scale pattern. From this courtyard the visitor has to turn sharply to the right in order to reach the heart of the villa, and in doing so he passes through a large rectangular vestibule (3). The figured mosaic panel in the centre of this room is now much destroyed, but it depicted two rows of richly clad figures, their hair bedecked with leaves and flowers (plate 56). Some of them hold laurel twigs or candles, and all incline their heads and eyes upwards to the right. The scene has been interpreted as some sort of welcoming ceremony *(adventus)*, but for whom has been much disputed (p. 90).

A broad gap at the far end of the vestibule leads directly to the central peristyle around which most of the villa's living quarters are arranged. In the middle is a large ornamental pool, and this was no doubt surrounded by a garden, but its present appearance is entirely fanciful and not based on the evidence of excavated bedding-trenches. The colonnade of granite, cipollino, and other marble columns, with Corinthian capitals, is laid out as an irregular rectangle, with 10 columns along the long sides and 8 along the short. The floor of the corridor around this is carpeted by a continuous series of animal- or bird-heads set within laurel wreaths; the wreaths in turn are positioned in a regular grid-pattern of guilloche squares (plate 4). Opposite the vestibule a small room (4) projects into the area of the garden. It has a geometric mosaic featuring an ivy leaf in the centre, and there is a pedestal in its apse flanked by columns. It was probably a household shrine.

At the north-west corner of the peristyle is the bath-suite, an elaborate complex of interlocking rooms with its axis at an oblique angle to the central block of the villa. It could be entered either direct from the entrance courtyard through the small rooms with geometrically patterned mosaic floors (5 and 7), or from the peristyle through a vestibule (13). The latter is decorated with a floor mosaic depicting a

5. Mosaic in the vestibule to the baths (room 13), showing a lady, her children and attendants

6. The large latrine near the baths, from the east

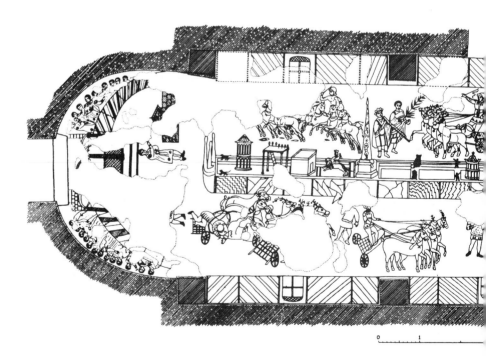

8. Drawing of the mosaic in room 8: chariot-racing in the Circus

7. The small latrine, from the south

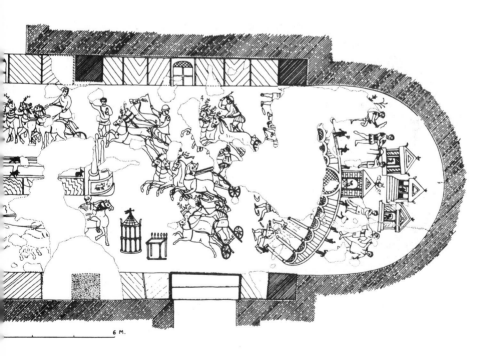

6 M.

lady, her two children and a pair of servants carrying a chest and box (plate 5). This was clearly the private entrance to the baths which the owner and his guests used from the villa itself, and it is reasonable to assume that the lady and children depicted in the mosaic are the wife and family of the owner *(dominus)* who commissioned the building and its decoration. The provision of a separate entrance (5 and 7) direct from the courtyard suggests that the baths were also available, at specific hours, for the owner's *clientela* from surrounding farms and villages, as well as for his own servants and their families, who could also enter 5 by a side door from the area round the back of the baths. The large semicircular latrine (6), also entered from here through a square vestibule, was probably likewise intended for them (plate 6). The seats were erected in customary fashion over a sewer and had a water channel for washing sponges (the Roman equivalent of toilet paper) in front of them. A semicircular mosaic-paved covered portico, its roof supported on brick columns, separated the seats from the tiny horseshoe-shaped court. By contrast the lavatory used by the owner and his guests (plate 7) was more conveniently reached direct from the peristyle across a triangular tile-paved yard (14). Here the seats face a figured mosaic floor, depicting a leopard, a mule, a hare and two birds on a white ground. There is no water-channel in front of the seats here, but hygiene was encouraged by the placing of a wash basin near the door.[13]

The first room of the bath-suite proper (8) is a double-apsed hall 22 m long with four columns along each wall. It is too grandiose to have been designed purely as an undressing room *(apodyterium)* – clothes may have been left in 7 or 13 – and it is usually interpreted as a *palaestra*, a covered hall where bathers could loosen up with a little exercise before proceeding to the actual baths. The mosaic here gives a splendidly detailed rendering of a chariot race in progress (plate 8).[14] The action takes place in the Circus Maximus in Rome, and the central *spina* is shown complete with obelisk and lap counter, as well as shrines and statues, including one of Cybele; there are also three conical pillars at each end to mark the turning points *(metae)*. In the right-hand (north) apse are depicted the starting-gates *(carceres)* for the chariots, behind which are three temples; the opposite apse is filled with chatting spectators. The chariot race itself is shown in three stages.[15] On the right four chariots (one of each of the four factions, White, Red, Green and Blue) are galloping spiritedly forward at the start of the race. At the left, both above and below the *spina*, the race is in mid course: the Green faction is in the lead, narrowly avoiding the 'shipwreck' *(naufragium)* which engulfs the Red charioteer in second place, while the Whites and the Blues trail behind and have not yet turned the corner. In the centre of the mosaic above the *spina* is the prize-giving ceremony: the victorious Green charioteer comes forward to receive a laurel branch to the accompaniment of a trumpet fanfare, and the chariot of the Reds trots up behind in second place (plate 59). The pair below the *spina* are probably meant to be seen as part of the same group, for the position of the horses' legs and the slackness of the reins show that they are merely processing at walking pace and not engaged in the hurly-burly of the race itself. Various cheer-leaders dressed in the colours of their respective factions and an umpire on horseback are also depicted on the circus track.

From here the bather passed into the *frigidarium*, an octagonal room with a continuous series of apses on all eight sides (9). Those on the east-west axis communicate with the adjacent rooms, while those on the north-south axis serve as plunge baths. The southern one is not semicircular but trefoil in plan, and the northern one is elongated to make room for a substantial pool. An arched aqueduct discharged water into this from a cistern 75 m to the north (plate 22). The mosaic of the *frigidarium* shows a marine scene of cupids fishing from four boats, a subject particularly popular at Piazza Armerina (cf. rooms 22, 31, 44 and 45), and the sea is swarming with nereids, tritons, centaurs and other assorted creatures (cf. room 32). Only two of the apse mosaics are well preserved. One shows a girl about to undress before her bath, the other a young man clad in a stole after the bath; each has a pair of

9. Furnace area for the *caldaria* of the baths, from the south-west

attendants at hand. A square cubicle (10) connects the western apse of the *frigidarium* with the heated rooms beyond. It may have been the room where bathers anointed themselves with oil prior to sweating in the steamy atmosphere of the *tepidarium* and *caldaria* beyond, as its mosaic shows a naked man being rubbed down by a brawny male attendant, while a companion alongside carries an oil flask and a strigil. A couple of slaves in the foreground complete the scene; their loin cloths name them as Titus and Cassius, and Cassius wears as well a strange, conical cap.

The warm room *(tepidarium*, 11) repeats the double-apse shape of the *palaestra*, but is smaller (18 m long), and along its west side are three hot rooms (*caldaria*, 12) of which two are equipped with small hot-water baths. The floors of all the heated rooms have vanished almost completely, exposing the *pilae* of the underfloor hypocaust heating

10. Geometric mosaic in room 18

system, but fragments of mosaic from the *tepidarium* suggest that the subject of its floor was a torch-race *(lampadedromia)*. These rooms were roofed by concrete barrel vaults and heated by five furnace-areas *(praefurnia)*, one for each of the *caldaria* (plate 9) and one at either end of the *tepidarium*. The furnaces were also roofed, with a vault consisting of interlocking tubular tiles.[16]

Of the group of rooms along the north side of the peristyle, only one (17A) is not floored with mosaic. Projecting out from the rear of the north wing, it possesses a bench along one side and a basin at one end; it could also be entered from the outside. An adjacent room (17) and another leading off it (16) both have geometric mosaic floors which are the simplest and least well-laid of the entire villa. This group of rooms may have been intended as the day quarters of servants on duty, from where they could be summoned to wait on the master, his family or their guests; and 17A may have been where food was kept warm on portable braziers, and other final touches were put to it before being taken to the dining-room. But this room is not the kitchen,[17] nor is there suitable accommodation in the villa as so far known for servants' sleeping quarters and other service rooms, stores and so on: these must lie elsewhere in a separate complex, yet to be located (p. 69).

Of the rest of the mosaics in this north wing, that in 19 has completely perished and those in 18 (see plate 10), 24 and 25 are elegant, polychrome geometric compositions. The floor in room 21 is also basically an all-over geometric design but incorporates circular medallions featuring busts of the four seasons, birds and fruit. Wholly figured compositions were laid in 20, 22 and 23. That in 20, which showed the highly unusual scene of couples dancing, is badly damaged. The floor of 22 depicts a lively group of cupid fishermen casting their nets and lines from four gaily coloured boats into a well-stocked sea; a porticoed seaside villa *(villa maritima)* lines the shore at the top (plate 33). The largest room in this wing of the villa (23) has one of the most celebrated of the Piazza Armerina mosaics, the composition known as the Small Hunt (plate 11). Here the hunting scenes are arranged in five registers around two central groups: a sacrifice to Diana before the hunt begins and an open-air picnic under an awning slung between the trees. The other, subsidiary scenes show beaters with their hounds in pursuit of foxes and hares; a captured boar slung upside down on a pole; bird-catching with glued lime-sticks and a decoy bird; the spearing of a hare lying concealed in a thicket by a man on horseback; and, at the bottom, the driving of deer into a net laid to ensnare them, and the killing of a wild boar who has already savaged one of the huntsmen: he lies bleeding on the ground while two other companions take refuge behind a rock.

The purpose of rooms 18–24 in this north wing of the villa is not immediately apparent. One or two, for example 18, may have been offices where the paperwork necessary for the running and upkeep of the villa was dealt with by a secretary or steward, but the rest must have been day-rooms and bedrooms, perhaps partly at least reserved for guests. Likewise the function of two of the three rooms bordering the south side of the peristyle corridor is not clear (37–8); both of them had geometric mosaics when the villa was first built (cf. below, p. 41). Room 39 has more pretensions, with an apse adorned by a statue of Apollo and a small fountain playing into a basin in the centre. Its floor, unfortunately much damaged, has one of the fullest and most detailed known representations of a theme very popular in antiquity, that of the animals being charmed by Orpheus with his lyre, who is here surrounded by a menagerie of no less than 45 creatures. It is possible that the room was used as a small private dining-room for the owner and his family when they were dining alone or at most with a few friends, and also for musical entertainments.

From the east end of the peristyle three flights of steps lead up to the transverse corridor (26), 70 m long, terminating in an apse at either end. This is carpeted throughout by the stupendous composition known as the Great Hunt, divided into three distinct parts (plate 12). At either end of the corridor a wide range of exotic animals, including a bull, an elephant, a hippopotamus, a rhinoceros, tigers, leopards, horses, goats, ostriches and so on (e.g. plates 35, 44, 58) are being lured into captivity by a variety of means: a leopard, for example, is tempted towards a trap-cage baited with a kid, and a fleeing huntsman on horseback who has stolen a tiger cub escapes from its enraged mother by dropping a convex mirror; the tigress, seeing a small reflection of herself, is momentarily deceived into thinking it one of her cubs. Other parts of the landscape are filled by felines pouncing on other animals, or by men pursuing similar prey, armed with swords and spears. The central portion of the floor shows a pair of boats being loaded with captured beasts on one side and simultaneously unloaded on the other, a neat device for depicting a sea voyage from start to finish. On the 'island' of land in the centre, receiving the cargo, are three officials wearing berets. Another man with similar headgear, who is accompanied by two attendants, is shown further to the right directing operations for capture (plate 54). We shall be hearing more about these figures in chapter three. The apse at either end depicts a personification; that on the north is almost entirely destroyed, but the mosaic in the south apse, showing a dark-skinned lady seated between an elephant and a tigress, is very well preserved (plate 13). The identification of these figures has been much disputed; but they may have been intended as generalized representations of the East and the West, indicating that the wild beasts shown here were gathered not just from one source but from all over the

11. Mosaic of the Small Hunt (room 23)

Roman Empire and beyond.[18] While mosaics with hunting scenes are common in the Roman world – in Italy, in Asia Minor and further east, and most especially in North Africa – no known composition can rival this huge mosaic at Piazza Armerina for its organizational skill, its variety and its restless vitality.[19]

Opening off the east side of the Great Hunt corridor is an enormous apsed hall, the so-called 'Basilica' (30), and two sets of mosaic-floored rooms. The hall, which measures 30 m by 14 m, is reached from the Great Hunt corridor up a flight of steps flanked by columns. The floor was paved in panels of cut polychrome marble *(opus sectile)*, but little is now in position except in the apse; there was also marble veneer on the walls. The roof of the hall was probably a conventional tiled one resting on timber rafters rather than a concrete barrel vault, but the apse had a semi-dome made of interlocking tubular tiles and was decorated in glittering vault mosaic of which a few scraps survived. The hall was probably designed for receptions, parties and banquets; it may also have served as an audience-hall for hearing petitions from clients (the *clientela*, p. 91).

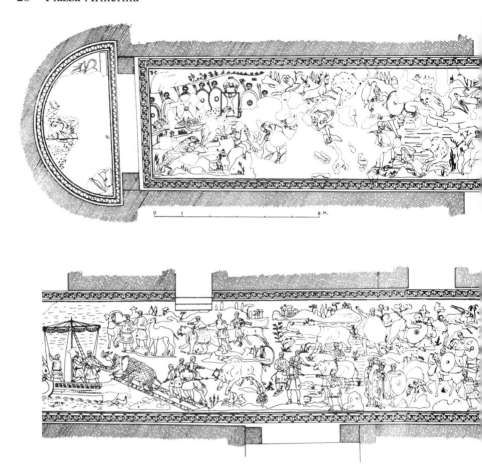

12. Drawing of the mosaic of the Great Hunt (26)

Of the flanking rooms the northern set may possibly have been the bedrooms of the master and his family. The Polyphemus and Ulysses story is the subject of the floor mosaic in 27: Ulysses carries a bowl of wine to the Cyclops in the cave while two companions prepare some more, but Polyphemus, gorging himself on the carcass of a ram, is curiously shown with pupils in all three eyes, not in one alone: the mosaicist can hardly have understood how impossible the subsequent blinding operation would have been had Ulysses three eyes to contend with rather than one (plate 14).[20] The other mosaics here depict baskets laden with different types of fruit (29), and a couple kissing (28; the surrounding medallions contain busts of the seasons and theatrical masks).

The southern set of rooms (plate 15), again richly floored, was surely

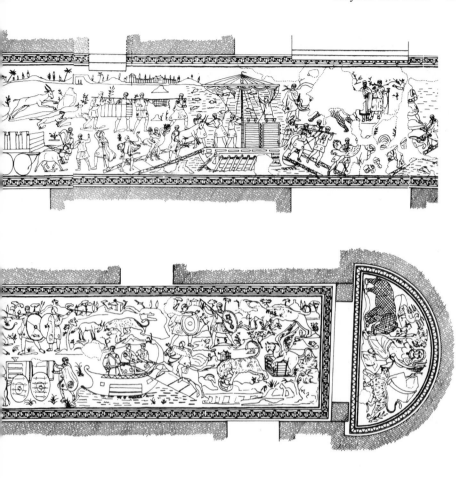

the private living suite of the owner and his family, set around its own semicircular court with a small fountain.[21] This little group has a delightful air of intimacy and self-containment which no other part of the villa displays. The mosaics here are especially charming. In the principal apsed living room (32) is a splendid gallery of sea-monsters and nereids disporting themselves with abandon around the central figure of Arion. It is an inventive, humorous display, with griffins and dragons, tigers and sea-panthers, hippocamps and bulls along with other fantastic creations crowding into a brimming sea. The horseshoe-shaped corridor separating this room from the fountain has another representation of cupids fishing. Equally playful are the delightful scenes of children hunting in room 36, driving bird-drawn chariots in a mock circus race (33) and acting or practising music (34). Rather more

13. Mosaic in the south apse of Great Hunt corridor ('The East'?)

14. Mosaic of Polyphemus and Ulysses (room 27)

enigmatic is the theme of the mosaic in 35, where Eros and Pan are about to engage in a wrestling or boxing match, with umpire alongside and an audience too; money bags and palm leaves in the background await the victor.

The final group of rooms lies on the south side of the main complex and was reached either by a door near the south-west angle of the peristyle, or else from one end of the Great Hunt corridor. The group consists of a great oval porticoed court (41) flanked by three small rooms on either side. The surviving mosaics here show cupids grape-harvesting (42) (plate 46), grape-pressing (43) and, yet again, fishing (44 and 45). Some portions also remain of the corridor floor, which was composed of a series of animal heads and foreparts *(protomai)* emerging from a continuous acanthus scroll (plate 37). But the focal point of this complex is the vast three-apsed hall *(triconchos,* 46) floored with magnificent, ambitious mosaics glorifying Hercules (plate 16). The hall is usually interpreted as a dining-room *(triclinium)*, presumably used only for banquets. The style of the mosaics here, especially in the central floor and in the eastern apse, is strikingly different from the compositions elsewhere at Piazza Armerina: not only do huge masses of flesh and drapery heave and twist in great contortions with a bold use of foreshortening,[22] but the scale of the figures is also much vaster than elsewhere in the villa. The central portion of the floor portrays the end-products, as it were, of Hercules' labours, the Carnage: the field is

15. The owner's living quarters (foreground) and the main peristyle beyond, seen from the east

16. Drawing of the mosaics in the *triconchos* (46)

6 M

strewn with dead or dying carcasses of the Marathonian bull, the Nemean lion, the Hydra of Lerna, the triple-bodied Geryon, and with Thracian riders falling from the grey mares of Diomedes. The northern (left) apse depicts the glorification of Hercules; in the eastern apse five giants writhe in their death-throes, felled by the poisoned arrows of Hercules; and in the south apse Ambrosia, about to be struck with a double axe by Lycurgus, is saved by her metamorphosis into a vine, with the help of Dionysus and his companions.

Other embellishments

The mosaic pavements are, of course, the most spectacular adornment of Piazza Armerina and they create a striking impression on the visitor today; yet they were only part of the decorative ensemble which also included marbles, frescoes and statuary. Unfortunately the fragmentary nature of these makes their original impact less readily experienced now. Columns of granite and marble are widely employed, sometimes for structural purposes, sometimes purely as grandiose decoration. Apart from the 32 columns of the peristyle, for example, they are used in the *palaestra* and *frigidarium* of the baths, in the 'Basilica' and in the *triconchos*, and to flank both entrance and apse of the main room in the private quarters (32). Marble flooring was used, as we have seen, in the 'Basilica', and marble wall veneer gave an added sumptuousness to that hall, as well as to rooms 32 and 39, to the corridor of the Great Hunt, and to the household shrine (4). The colour, range and diversity of marbles used at Piazza Armerina are truly astonishing, and all the major marble-producing areas of the Roman world are well represented. They include not only common stones such as yellow marble *(giallo antico)* from North Africa, green porphyry from Greece, cipollino (for many of the columns) from the island of Euboea and white Proconnesian marble from north-west Asia Minor (for the capitals), but also rarer marbles from Africa, Greece, Asia Minor and elsewhere.[23] The list is an impressive one, a vivid witness to the wealth and taste of the villa's owner. Some of the veneers are certainly re-used material, for two of the marbles (*lumachella* from Egypt and *madreponte rossa* from Asia Minor) are otherwise known only in first-century contexts. Presumably most or all of these came from a marble stockist in Italy, probably at Rome, although some of the African marbles may have come from a depot in a Sicilian port trading with that continent, such as Syracuse or Agrigento. At any rate most of the marbles at Piazza Armerina were certainly not in common circulation in Sicily.

Where marble veneers were not employed, the walls were decorated with frescoes, and because the stonework is regularly preserved to a height of about two metres some considerable traces of this fresco work have survived, although none of it has ever been published in detail. These paintings were not sober and restrained works avoiding competition with the riotous floor decoration: the blaze of polychrome and figured composition was continued on the walls as well. A few examples may give some idea. In room 22, where the mosaic floor shows cupids fishing, the wall scheme consists of a dado with black swastikas and, above, red-bordered rectangular panels on a brilliant yellow ground. The panels are alternately broad and narrow; the broader ones each contained a female figure, now largely destroyed, on a white or pale blue ground. Of the wall painting in room 36, where the mosaic depicts children hunting, a standing female figure is particularly striking: she wears a rich red and yellow gown, edged in darker red, and holds a basket, while a companion looks on. The ground is pale blue. In the apse of room 28 (the main room has the 'kissing couple' mosaic, but the apse floor consists of a geometric design of intersecting circles), the wall painting consists of a dado of purple ovals on a red ground with black strips at intervals, and a main field of narrow and broad panels as in room 22. The narrow panels are outlined in yellow and have a plain red strip in the centre; the broad ones contain a diamond outlined in red, in each of which is a single figure. The best-preserved is a pink-clad dancing girl whirling a purple scarf above her head, a scene which also appears in mosaic in room 20. It would appear from these examples that the subject matter of mosaic and fresco in the same room was normally unrelated, and that the 'all-over' style of the floors was not repeated on the walls. A full publication of the frescoes at Piazza Armerina is highly desirable; they add an extra dimension, hitherto neglected, to the interior decoration of this sumptuous mansion.[24] The outside walls, too, were given a plaster rendering, but here few traces of painted designs survive.[25]

One final touch of affluence remains to be mentioned. As was customary in any rich patrician residence from the late Republic onwards, the villa was embellished with statues. In some cases no more than a few fragments survive, but the evidence points to a statue of Venus in an antechamber of the baths (5), of Apollo in room 39, of a cherub holding a dove possibly from the fountain in the garden court (15), and a larger than life-size statue, variously interpreted as Hercules or an emperor, in the apse of the 'Basilica' (30). A male head, and fragments of feet and hands belonging to other sculptures, have also been recovered; pedestals in the shrine (4) and the three-apsed hall (46) were doubtless designed to take further statues. Apart from the Corinthian capitals, there was a cornice decorated with architectural ornament above the entrance to the 'Basilica', and a few other scraps of marble pilaster capitals also survive.

The date of Piazza Armerina

So much, then, for the bare facts. We have here a very large and very opulent building-complex spread over an area of 150 m by 100 m (1½ hectares), adorned with expensive, gaudy polychrome mosaics, nearly all of them figured, and with paintings or marble veneer on the walls; a building too with playing fountains, with statuary, with a spacious bath-suite, and with magnificent halls for entertainment on the grand scale. This much is tangible evidence. But the questions posed by the mansion are numerous and difficult; and it is some of these problems, and possible solutions for them, that we shall be considering in the rest of this book.

The first problem concerns the date. The villa just described was not the earliest building to have been erected on this site. The main excavations of the 1950s, and again the trenches cut in 1970, made it clear that there was an earlier villa here, erected either at the end of the first or, more probably, some time during the second century AD. Regrettably all too little is known about it. Fragments of it have been located at various points: walling under the 'Basilica' (30) and the peristyle corridor (15), an *opus signinum* floor under the oval court (41), and an apsed heated room belonging to a bath-suite under the Circus mosaic in room 8. Nothing coherent is therefore known of its plan but one highly significant fact emerges: that the earlier villa appears to have covered an area no less extensive than its successor. At any rate it was totally demolished when the visible mansion was erected.

Quite when that was has not been as clearly established as it should have been. It has been stated above that the villa was built in the first or second decade of the fourth century, and the evidence for that date must now be examined, as well as theories that the visible villa is a multi-period structure rather than the product of a single building plan.

In the almost complete absence of any published archaeological evidence from the 1950–4 excavations, discussion was centred for almost twenty years on the stylistic elements of the mosaics themselves. For Biagio Pace the 'period to which belong all the possible parallels' was the latter part of the fourth century AD and the beginning of the fifth.[26] For Cagiano de Azevedo, another proponent of this dating, the best parallels for the mosaics of Piazza Armerina were the floors of Mopsuestia in Cilicia (Asia Minor), datable between 392 and 428, but the dissimilarities between the two are more striking than the similarities.[27] Carandini, on the other hand, in a long art-historical study published in 1964, marshalled a great number of parallels in the mosaics of North Africa and Italy and suggested a dating between *c.* 320 and *c.* 370;[28] but the chronology of the African mosaics is itself notoriously shaky and his later work, as we shall see, caused a revision of this dating.

17. The Circus mosaic in room 8, detail of obelisk

Other scholars have argued about the importance of the position of the obelisk (plate 17) in the Circus Maximus mosaic of the baths: it appears on the *spina* but off-centre. For Ragona this represents the obelisk which the emperor Constantius II raised in 357, because of the flaming torch at its summit which the historian Ammianus Marcellinus says that it had;[29] but according to another ancient writer that was the normal finish to any obelisk, and a second-century relief of the Circus Maximus appears to show one.[30] For Nash, the Circus mosaic depicts Augustus' obelisk, but was executed after 326, when Constantine took the decision to erect a second one and allegedly moved Augustus' obelisk from its central position on the *spina* to make room for it (hence its off-centre siting on the mosaic); and before 357, when the project was finally completed and Constantius' obelisk was raised in the middle of the Circus.[31] There is, however, no ancient evidence that Augustus' obelisk was ever actually moved, and its off-centre position might have been caused by later enlargements of the *spina*. More importantly, the real position of the obelisk was surely only a matter of secondary importance to the designer of the Piazza Armerina mosaic, who was more concerned with giving prominence to the victorious charioteer and his reception than with the historical accuracy of the embellishments of the *spina*. The precise positioning of this obelisk has thus proved a somewhat fruitless line of enquiry for the dating of the Piazza Armerina mosaics.[32]

The archaeological evidence for the chronology of the villa from the major excavation campaigns of Gentili has, unfortunately, never been satisfactorily recorded. Coins found beneath the mosaics belonged mostly to the second half of the third century, and likewise the pottery has been declared to be 'pre-Constantinian'. Above the mosaics were found coins of Maxentius (306–12) and the second Flavians (312–63). But the 'most important factor' according to Gentili was the discovery of a coin of Maximian, of the last years of the third century, 'in the mortar which cemented the marble slab of the threshold in the south-east exedra of the *frigidarium*'.[33] Obviously a single 'stratified' coin, without even any published information as to its state of wear, is no more than a very vague dating indicator.

The unsatisfactory nature of this evidence prompted Carandini to dig a few small trial trenches in order to try and secure a more reliable chronology. The levels associated with the construction of the late-Roman villa yielded third-century coins, and some pieces of African red slip pottery belonging to the type classed by Lamboglia as *terra sigillata chiara D*; none of it had stamped decoration, and there were no African-made lamps in these levels.[34] Excavation elsewhere, notably in North Africa, has now provided reasonably secure evidence that this type of pottery and this class of lamps did not make an appearance before *c*. 300, nor the stamped ware before *c*. 320/25.[35] The chronology of the villa would now therefore appear to be fairly well fixed within the first quarter of the fourth century AD, although it must be stressed that the sample of stratified archaeological material recovered by Carandini was very small. The trenches were, moreover, limited to only a very few areas, mostly in the peristyle garden (15) and the great hall or 'Basilica' (30). Is it possible that other parts of the villa belong not to the same period but to widely differing ones?

Some scholars have interpreted the unorthodox layout of the villa, with its ever-shifting axes, as a sign that there were several changes of plan and that construction work was spread out over several decades. Lugli, for example, in making a careful study of the various structural abutments (straight joints) of one part of the building with another, came to the conclusion that the baths were built first (*c*. 280–300), followed by the main complex of peristyle and surrounding rooms (*c*. 300–30); and that the oval court and *triconchos* were added considerably

18. The oval court (41) seen from the *triconchos*

later (c. 350–70), with the 'Basilica' not being built until c. 370–80.[36] The dating evidence for this sequence was negligible, and the contemporary date of the great hall with the rest of the peristyle complex has now been indicated by Carandini's work. More recently Kähler has argued, again from structural abutments, that the baths are later than the peristyle complex, and that the entrance court, together with rooms 5 and 7, are later than both.[37] But he also realized – and this is the important point – from both the uniformity of mosaic style and the presence of external plaster-rendering which covers the abutments, that the building periods were not separated by any considerable lengths of time from one another. There were, of course, some changes which were no doubt made during construction, and some parts of the villa were completed before others, as various structural abutments undoubtedly demonstrate; but for a country villa of this size and richness to be planned, for example, without a bath-suite is inconceivable, and such a complex must have been on the drawing board from the start. To suppose from the lack of axial symmetry that the different elements belong to different periods is to miss an essential feature of the architecture of Piazza Armerina.[38] It is a carefully contrived essay in relaxed sprawl, deliberately avoiding the predictable regularity of the normal peristyle house, where an uninterrupted vista was often possible from the entrance to the back of the dwelling. At Piazza Armerina that never happens: the axis of the entrance court is nearly at right angles to the peristyle; the view from the vestibule (3) across the garden of the peristyle is blocked by the small shrine (4); and the axis of the great hall (30) has been shifted slightly from that of the peristyle. The baths and the *triconchos* (46) follow independent axes of their own; and the view from the latter, instead of commanding a pleasant tract of peaceful, wooded valley, is blocked off by a high, niche-relieved wall at the far end of the oval court (plate 18). All this is not accidental but the product of deliberate overall planning: it reflects an introspection, a desire for seclusion on the part of the owner, for its inward-turning nature, while characteristic of some late-Roman architecture, does not appear to be a widespread feature of fourth-century country mansions elsewhere in the Roman world (see below further, pp. 73–85).

It has also been supposed by some scholars that the *triconchos* (46), oval court (41) and flanking rooms (42–5) represent an afterthought sometime later than the original villa.[39] From an architectural point of view this complex could, strictly speaking, be regarded as an 'optional extra', in that a hall suitable for banquets already existed in the villa (30) and the provision of an extra one, if that indeed is what room 46 was designed for, might be regarded as superfluous; instead it may have been the original intention to complete the south side of the peristyle with a more or less regular set of rooms. Certainly there is a structural abutment between 42 and 39, and the only doorways giving access from the heart of the villa to the oval court, near the south apse of the Great Hunt corridor and at the south-west end of the peristyle corridor, are undoubtedly secondary insertions; but there is no hint that any fourth-century structures on the south-west side of the peristyle needed to be demolished to make room for the oval court and *triconchos*.[40] In fact, it seems most unlikely that the complex of rooms 41–6 is other than contemporary with the rest of the villa. In particular the cupid mosaics in rooms 42–5 are identical in style to those with the same theme elsewhere in the villa and must have been laid at the same time. What has misled scholars is the totally different creations of the mosaicists who worked in the *triconchos*, but, as we shall see in the next chapter, there are no good grounds for thinking these mosaics as well are other than contemporary. If the *triconchos* with its court was an afterthought, as the secondary doorways from 15 and 26 suggest, it seems very likely that it was an afterthought which occurred while the rest of the villa was still a-building, and not years later.[41]

The later history of the site

About the subsequent fortunes of the villa after its completion in the first quarter of the fourth century, very little is unfortunately known, as the evidence was largely removed without proper record during the

19. Mosaic repairs in the *frigidarium*

excavations of the 1950s. A few points are, however, clear. Various minor repairs and alterations can be detected, as in room 36, for example, where the original fresco on the walls was covered by marble veneer at some secondary period; similarly the white tessellation which originally lined the pools in both *frigidarium* (8) and *caldaria* (12) of the baths was later covered with marble slabs. The mosaic floors also show many signs of minor repair, such as the use of larger *tesserae*, *opus signinum* or marble chips to fill in small holes.[42] The popularity of the baths, however, and the faster deterioration of its floors, required more drastic work: in the *frigidarium*, for example, some of the fish and dolphins have been crudely and clumsily redrawn by a later hand (plate 19), and larger *tesserae* were also used to patch up two of the figures in the adjacent cubicle (10). There were also extensive repairs, including new and not disastrously inferior figure work, in the centre of the Great Hunt corridor (plate 20),[43] and the portion in front of the central steps of the peristyle corridor was completely relaid with a new design, including one panel showing millet stalks and the name Bonufatius, and another depicting poorly drawn ivy-leaves springing from a chalice. Gentili thought that this work was Byzantine, but it need not be later than the

20. Mosaic repairs in the Great
    Hunt corridor

21. Mosaic of the bikini girls (room 38), with an earlier geometric floor beneath

end of the fourth century or thereabouts.[44] On a rather larger scale, however, were entirely fresh compositions laid in one of the *frigidarium* apses (a dressing scene) and in room 38. The mosaic in the latter, which covered an original floor of geometric design, is one of the most photographed though technically one of the least accomplished compositions in the entire villa. This is the celebrated 'bikini' maidens mosaic, where the girls appear to be engaged in various kinds of athletic competition involving balls, dumbells, tambourines and miniature wheels (plate 21).[45] When and why this mosaic was laid is unknown. Stylistically it need be no later than the mid fourth century, and if some practical reason such as rising damp demanded the laying of a fresh floor it need not be very much later (perhaps a decade or so) than the rest of the mosaics at Piazza Armerina.[46]

Few other major alterations can be detected. The most significant[47] is the addition of masonry reinforcement piers behind the apse of the great hall (30), and at the northern ends of the Great Hunt corridor (26), of the *palaestra* (8) and of the cold plunge-bath; the arches of the aqueduct, too, were blocked up at a secondary period (plate 22). All this suggests major structural damage, possibly inflicted by an earthquake in AD 365, when other parts of Sicily are known to have suffered.[48] But the gravest lacuna about the later history of the site concerns our ignorance about how long the villa was maintained as a residence of elegance and sophistication.[49] Gentili implies that occupa-

22. The northern aqueduct heading for the baths, from the west

tion was continuous until the eighth century at least, but the mosaics will
not have survived the wear and tear of four centuries and they must by
then have long been covered with rubbish and earth. This squatter
occupation appears to have come to an end c. 800, possibly after a fire,[50]
and there was then a gap in occupation before the ruins of the villa
became the nucleus of a village under the Normans about the year 1000.
Known as Platia (derived from the Latin *palatium*, 'palace'), it continued in use until 1161 AD, when the site was abandoned and the
modern town of Piazza Armerina founded. Byzantine, Arab and
Norman glazed pottery have all been recorded from the site, as well as
coins of the Byzantine emperors Heraclius (610–41) and Constantine II
(654–9), and of the Norman kings too, down to Roger II (1130–54). But
whether we should ascribe the walls which were built among the ruins,
and which were recorded before their removal in the 1940s and 1950s
(plate 23), to the Byzantine, Arab or Norman periods, is not altogether
clear. Most of the damage done to the mosaics by pit-digging, for
example in rooms 10, 21 and 24, was attributed by Gentili to the
Normans, and a pottery kiln (plate 24) also of Norman date, was built in
room 16. In room 19 the Roman mosaic had been destroyed and
replaced by a rough slab floor at some period before Norman times, and
tombs were built in and around the apsed great hall (30). Byzantine,
Arab and Norman activity is, therefore, documented down to the
twelfth century, with apparently a gap about 800–1000. But we still do
not know when the standard of civilized living at the villa declined into
squatter occupation. The great mansion may have been maintained for
perhaps 150 years, at most until the early sixth century: but that is no
more than a guess.

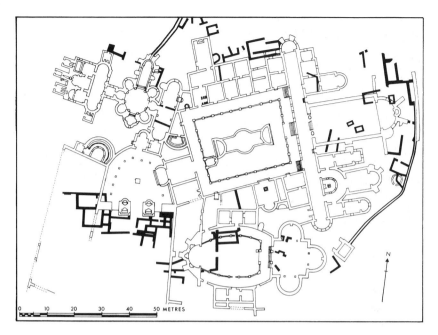

23. Plan of the villa, showing Byzantine, Arab and Norman additions (in solid black)

24. Norman kiln inserted in room 16

Chapter Two
Mosaics and Mosaicists

The mosaics at Piazza Armerina are the most striking feature of the villa today: they make a stunning impact, not so much because of their artistic quality (the standard is at times abysmally low) as for the sheer quantity of them, the variety of the figured composition, and the richness of the polychromy. The terse descriptions and illustrations in chapter one may have given some idea of their variety and complexity; but while fuller details of each floor would be out of place in this short account, some wider questions which are raised by the whole vast area of mosaic flooring must not go unasked. In particular we must enquire whence came the inspiration for the designs employed; how long the entire project took to complete and whether there is evidence from the floors themselves of a considerable time-lag between commencement and completion; whether we should speak of one or more master craftsmen as responsible for each overall composition; and, if more than one, whether they belonged to a single very productive mosaic work-shop, or whether we must view the Piazza Armerina mosaics as the corporate products of several different and normally competing firms.

To provide answers to all these questions is extremely difficult; indeed in the present state of our knowledge about the organization of the mosaic industry of antiquity it would be rash to attempt definitive conclusions. Only one of the queries can be answered positively: that concerning the source of the subject matter at Piazza Armerina. Not only is there no adequate evidence from Sicily for supposing that a local mosaic firm was capable of responding to what one assumes was the exceptional commission placed by the owner of our villa; but it is more than clear, thanks to the detailed researches of several scholars,[1] that floor after floor at Piazza Armerina have parallels, often extremely close parallels, in the rich and varied legacy of mosaic paving that the Roman provinces of North Africa have bequeathed to us. A few of the more striking of these parallels will be indicated in turn below. It is beyond all reasonable doubt that the pavements of Piazza Armerina were laid, not by local workmen struggling to master African-inspired blueprints, but by actual squads of African mosaicists imported into the province to carry out this contract. Indeed Gentili has indicated that most of the *tesserae* used at Piazza Armerina are made of African, not Sicilian, stones.[2]

25. Mosaic in room 28, kissing couple

Mosaic designers

Much more controversial is the number of different artistic 'personalities' which are to be identified as having worked on the extant floors. Several scholars have drawn up elaborate theories about individual 'masters' who created the designs for this or that group of mosaics, and some of these ideas will be explored in more detail below. One of the most closely argued analyses, for example, by Wladimiro Dorigo, postulated the existence of five principal 'masters' at work in the villa, each a distinctive personality.[3] Other writers, on the other hand, have claimed that such an approach is completely misguided. Andrea Carandini, for example, in his analysis of the Great Hunt mosaic, saw that particular floor as a group of separate components placed together by different sets of workmen without any strong guiding personality.[4]

The truth surely lies somewhere between the two. There seems little doubt that all the mosaic workshops of antiquity used copybooks which contained a wide range of sketches showing stock motifs and designs, and some, perhaps indeed most, of the motifs which occur at Piazza Armerina were so derived. To that extent it is misleading to speak of 'master artists', for a mosaic designer or craftsman did not normally produce a wholly original floor in the way in which a canvas painter produces an 'original' masterpiece. But at the same time the complicated compositions of the Piazza Armerina floors must have required

26. Carthage, mosaic of the boar hunt (*Musée du Bardo*)

one or more master designers of great dexterity, who were responsible
for preparing the overall composition of each floor in advance, drawing
on some already familiar motifs but no doubt newly composing others.
Each designer or, if a different person, as seems likely, a master
craftsman who worked closely with him,[5] would then have supervised
the mosaicists employed in his workshop in the process of laying and
executing the mosaic.[6] The corridor of the Great Hunt is only one of the
more obvious cases in point. Many of the individual scenes here, of lion
preying on antelope, of armed man attacking feline, of boar trussed up
and carried on a pole, and so on, can be paralleled on numerous mosaics
found over a wide area of the African continent and indeed beyond,[7]
and were clearly part of the stock-in-trade of any mosaic firm composing
a hunting scene. But the process of selecting such episodes, of composing new variations, of placing them and marshalling them into a
tightly-knit overall composition required a master designer of outstanding ability who must have worked with this particular corridor at Piazza
Armerina entirely in mind.

There remains, however, the problem of estimating how many such
designers worked on the mosaics as a whole. It seems reasonable to

27. El Djem, mosaic of the hare hunt (*Musée du Bardo*)

assume, given the number of floors involved, that several different hands were responsible for preparing the original cartoons for the entire villa; but the fact that four different scholars have proposed four completely different classifications about the 'style' of the mosaics and the 'masters' who designed them is enough to underline the difficulties involved and the unlikelihood of neat solutions. Gentili, for example, identifies three different designers. One, he thinks, was responsible for the *triconchos* (46) and the south sector of the Great Hunt, as well as the Polyphemus and Ulysses floor (27), Arion (32) and other marine scenes; he claims that the figures here follow the traditional 'classical' forms of naturalism. To a second designer, who had a similar feeling for naturalistic forms but preferred an arrangement by register, he assigns the mosaics in room 3 (the *adventus* scene), 20 (dancers), 36 (boys hunting) and 34 (boy musicians and actors). The rest of the floors are, claims Gentili, the work of a third 'artist', 'undoubtedly talented but not exceptionally so': he was responsible for the rest of the Great Hunt (26), the Small Hunt (23), both circus races (8 and 33) and several others.[8] The grounds for this classification appear to be minimal, based on arbitrary and unconvincing principles of personal taste; in particular the conception that the Great Hunt corridor betrays evidence of two quite different designers seems particularly wayward. Cagiano de Azevedo, in a much more limited analysis, prefers to see a different designer for each of the largest compositions, the Hercules cycle (46), the Small Hunt (23), the Great Hunt (26) and the Circus (8).[9] Yet another scholar, Wladimiro Dorigo, on the other hand, sees the last three floors as the work of one great designer ('The Hunt Master'), while the creator of the Hercules scenes ('The Carnage Master') he rightly dubs as a man of 'truly innovating creative audacity'.[10] To these Dorigo adds a third master designer ('The Court Master') responsible for all the cupid and marine scenes (9, 22, 31, 32, 42–5), as well as others with a light or playful touch, such as the children sequence in rooms 33, 34 and 36, the Orpheus scene of 39, and the kissing couple mosaic (28) (plate 25) and adjacent floors. He points to a refined, elegant and often humorous style as well as a great attention to detail, which are common to the whole group.[11] The animal heads of the peristyle (15), however, he ascribes to a different hand (the 'Master of the Heads'), and he similarly maintains, and quite rightly, that the bikini girls (38) are composed by another designer, as this figured floor is undoubtedly later than the rest.

It will be seen from this brief summary that scholarly opinions differ widely on the number of master designers who were responsible for the cartoons on which the villa floors were based, or even which groups of mosaics most likely belong together. The possibilities are endless and opinions largely subjective; it is a line of enquiry with no clear definitions. It seems likely enough that several different designers, not just one man, drew up the schemata for the decoration of each floor in close consultation with the patron; that both Hunting mosaics, with similar use of landscape and the same techniques of registers and ground lines,[12] were designed by one man; that the group of fishing cupids, marine scenes and children playing has a homogeneous charm about it which suggests also the work of a single, and most probably different, designer; and that the compositions of the *triconchos* are the work of a separate hand altogether. Further than that it is unwise to speculate. At least three, and possibly several more, master designers probably worked on the cartoons which formed the basis for equipping the mansion at Piazza Armerina with its rich and varied carpet of mosaic decoration.

About such cartoon sketches and the amount of detail shown in them we have tantalizingly little information. We do not know if they were on papyrus or parchment (which were expensive but would allow for detailed drawings) or simply on cloth or canvas, nor do we understand precisely how the ideas were transmitted from 'paper' to floor. The mortar bed on which the mosaic rested was probably painted with at least the bare guidelines of the mosaic composition to be laid above,

28. Dermech, mosaic showing the capture and transport of animals, detail (*Musée de Carthage*)

much as Renaissance frescoes were guided by preparatory *sinopie*, but such evidence has not been sought at Piazza Armerina, nor has it been widely detected elsewhere in the ancient world.[13] The most competent mosaicists were then set to work on the principal figures, the more inexperienced craftsmen being allotted the less important parts of the floor;[14] and the routine filling-in work of the plain (normally white) background *tesserae* was presumably entrusted to raw apprentices. But quite how the various squads of *tessellarii* were organized is still not fully understood.[15]

Nor can we accurately gauge how long it would have taken to finish all the 3,500 sq m of mosaic flooring at Piazza Armerina, assuming that all were laid as part of one continuous, uninterrupted programme. Pace's estimate, based on the rate at which modern restorers worked at the villa, was that the mosaics were laid over a period of half a century, but

29. Piazza Armerina, detail of mosaic in room 36, boy hunting

this opinion has now justly been discarded.[16] Not only could we expect a far greater diversity of styles in the mosaics than is in fact apparent; but it is also obvious that no owner's patience could be tried for so long. He would surely want to see his project completed within five to ten years at the very most, and there seems no reason why what must have been a well organized and highly developed industry in North Africa could not have responded to his needs and completed the entire floor decoration in a comparatively short period of time.

One other possibility which may have greatly helped the smooth completion of the entire mosaic project should also be borne in mind. The logistic problems involved in marshalling, housing and feeding squads of mosaicists brought over from North Africa must have been considerable, problems which could have been alleviated if some panels were prefabricated in the base workshop and transported ready-made to the site. How widespread was the practice of prefabricating mosaics in antiquity is far from clear.[17] In the case of Piazza Armerina most of the 'all-over' compositions were probably unsuited for this method of production; nor does it seem likely that really large prefabricated mosaic panels would have survived the crating-up, shipment overseas and then a final laborious journey in waggons on a bumpy road to a site which lies almost as far from the sea as is possible in Sicily. Nevertheless, some panels, for example the component parts of geometric mosaics, or the animal heads of the peristyle, may possibly have been

30. Carthage, Maison des Chevaux, detail of mosaic showing boy hunting

transported in this way, and evidence for prefabrication (especially differences in the colour of the bedding mortar) should be carefully sought if and when more of the floors are lifted prior to consolidation.[18]

How many mosaic 'schools'?

If we accept the hypothesis that several different master designers worked at Piazza Armerina, need we assume that each came from a separate 'school' of mosaicists and that several different workshops *(officinae)* were called upon simultaneously to execute the floor mosaics? The problem of identifying individual teams of craftsmen working on the mosaics is an enormous one, fraught with difficulties. Despite the vast amount of material known in North Africa little work has so far been done on the identification of idiosyncracies of style and motif which might be assignable to individual workshops.[19] We simply do not know enough about the extent to which patterns and copybooks were circulated among rival *officinae*. There was no law of copyright in antiquity and this presumably gave room for some borrowing of other firms' ideas. Certainly the clues to originality are not to be sought in the stock figure-scenes which occur in such profusion that they must have been the common material of mosaic designers in many different workshops, separated from each other both geographically and chronologically; but rather in the smaller, idiosyncratic variations of such

31. Carthage, Maison des Chevaux, detail of mosaic showing boy lassoing a duck

scenes or in distinctive ornamental motifs. The geometric mosaics in particular, so far largely ignored in North Africa (as indeed at Piazza Armerina), are likely to prove fertile ground for isolating individual workshop preferences. As for the number of firms productive at any one time, we have no real idea. The sheer quantity of mosaics suggests that there must have been several working in Africa Proconsularis (roughly modern Tunisia) alone, perhaps in every big city. Carthage, as one of ths most prosperous provincial capitals of late antiquity, must have supported a number of workshops, but their relationship with *ateliers* in other prosperous towns awaits more detailed study: in many places there were probably branch workshops which were offshoots from a parent company in the capital. Let us now examine in turn some of the mosaics at Piazza Armerina and consider more closely their relationship to the North African series.

The two Hunting mosaics, as already mentioned, have many elements familiar from the African repertoire. Scenes such as the hare in a thicket, the man setting off with his dogs, or the captured boar slung on the underside of a pole were probably stock motifs common to many workshops: they can be seen, to take only two well-known examples, in the Boar Hunt mosaic from Carthage (plate 26) and the Hare Hunt from El Djem (plate 27), both belonging to the third century.[20] The arrangement of scenes by registers on these floors also recalls the Small Hunt at Piazza Armerina. Many other scenes from the latter mosaic, such as the deer being driven into a net, the spearing of the boar or the sacrifice before the hunt, can be paralleled on other African floors.

The motif of the boar being carried on a pole also occurs on the Great Hunt at Piazza Armerina, but until quite recently precise African parallels for other scenes in this stupendous composition have been

32. Piazza Armerina, detail of mosaic in room 36, boy lassoing a duck

lacking. The closest comparison was with the mosaic at Hippo Regius (Bône, Algeria) where the baited trap-cage and the large ox-cart also appear.[21] The style is very different but the scenes are probably based, ultimately, on the same copybook sketch. Some splendid animal scenes from Cherchel, farther west on the Algerian coast, have also been compared with those of the Great Hunt at Piazza Armerina, but the stiffer, more stylized composition suggests they belong somewhat later (probably to the mid or late fourth century).[22] These comparisons led Carandini to suggest that whereas the Small Hunt (and other mosaics) seemed to derive from Carthaginian workshops, the Great Hunt owed its inspiration more to Numidia and Mauretania.[23] But discoveries at Carthage during the 1960s have made it highly probable that the Great Hunt was also the work of Carthaginian mosaicists. Scenes of combat between men and animals from the Maison des Chevaux there, even though less skilfully drawn than the rounded, fluent creatures of the Piazza Armerina Great Hunt, were probably based on the same copybook sketches; and an even more compelling parallel is provided by the Dermech hunt at Carthage, where a remarkable number of the scenes are more or less closely matched at Piazza Armerina.[24] These include not only the standard hunting scene set-pieces (man spearing a leopard, man spearing a boar, lion seizing a horse, leopard leaping on its prey and so on), but also other episodes such as the boar suspended from a pole, the lioness approaching a baited trap, and the horseman escaping with an animal cub from its enraged mother up the gang-plank of a ship (plate 28). Some of these were stock motifs circulating widely in the mosaicists' copybooks, but the combination of so many compar-able scenes in both the Dermech floor and the Piazza Armerina Great Hunt, as well as a close similarity (and not just a general resemblance)

33. Mosaic in room 22, cupids fishing

34. Carthage, mosaic of cupids fishing (*Musée du Bardo*)

35. Piazza Armerina, Great Hunt mosaic, elephant boarding a ship (detail)

in style, strongly suggests that both floors are the product of the same workshop. The Dermech hunt was believed by its excavator, on the grounds of greater realism and the more excited, intense expressions of those taking part, to be slightly earlier than the Piazza Armerina Great Hunt.[25] Such stylistic judgments must always be treated with caution, for variations might as easily be due to differing standards of craftsmanship as to different dates. But if the Dermech hunt is indeed earlier, then it has repercussions on the dating of Piazza Armerina. Two coins of the emperor Maximian of AD 297–302, one only slightly worn, were found in the makeup under the Dermech hunt mosaic, and suggest that the floor was probably laid in the first few years of the fourth century. The Great Hunt at Piazza Armerina may, therefore, have been composed *c.* 310/15, a date consistent with the chronology proposed above (pp. 36–7).

Apart from the hunting scenes already mentioned the Maison des Chevaux at Carthage has produced what is perhaps the most compelling parallel of all between the North African floors and those at Piazza Armerina. Some of the episodes in the charming mosaic of boys hunting which decorates room 36 of our villa are precisely matched on the border strip in the main salon of the Carthage house. On both floors are depicted the same kind of fruit trees, infested with birds, and the same kind of garlands; and the hunting scenes themselves have only the slightest differences. At Piazza Armerina (plate 29) it is a hare that is being speared, at Carthage, in successive scenes, it is a young leopard (plate 30) and a small cat: at Carthage (plate 31) an unsuspecting duck is about to be lassoed (the episode is depicted twice), whereas at Piazza Armerina (plate 32) the deed is done and the duck is flapping her wings. Even if the two mosaics are not exactly contemporary,[26] there are few other African floors which more vividly or precisely demonstrate the

36.   Thuburbo Maius, mosaic of animal *protomai* (*Musée du Bardo*)

37. Piazza Armerina, mosaic in the corridor of the oval peristyle

close ties between that continent and the Sicilian villa. Furthermore if we assume, as is reasonable, that both the children hunting and the animal scenes in the Maison des Chevaux at Carthage were laid at the same time by the same workshop,[27] then it is logical to assume also that the mosaicists at Piazza Armerina who laid the 'Children Hunting' floor and the other closely comparable mosaics in the same group (cf. p. 48) also belonged to the same firm as those who executed the Great Hunt and the Small Hunt.

Another of the more appealing themes at Piazza Armerina is that of cupids fishing: playfully casting their lines and nets from gaily painted boats they sport themselves on no less than five floors in the villa. The subject occurs almost *ad nauseam* in the African mosaic repertoire, as well as elsewhere, but four of the Piazza Armerina mosaics have an additional, and distinctive, feature of a porticoed seaside villa *(villa maritima)* decorating the top edge of the composition (plate 33). Buildings do obtrude occasionally in these scenes in North Africa, but the closest parallel of a fishing scene with a *villa maritima* along the top edge occurs on a mosaic in the Bardo at Tunis which comes, once again, from Carthage (plate 34).[28] That the Piazza Armerina Arion sea-monster mosaic (32) should be ascribed to the same group as the fishing cupid floors in the villa (9, 22, 31, 44 and 45) is beyond all reasonable doubt – there is a self-evident link in the mosaic of room 9, where fishing cupids and sea-monsters rub shoulders on the same floor[29] – and if it is accepted that the children scenes are all part of the same homogeneous group, as Dorigo has cogently argued (p. 48), then the number of floors which should probably be ascribed to the same workshop grows still greater. Additional indications of links between the floors can be sought from small details. Compare, for example, the decorative boats used by the fishing cupids in 22 with the one transporting animals on the Great Hunt corridor (plates 33 and 35), or in the Carthage Dermech mosaic (plate 28): it is hard to assume from these that one is dealing other than with the craftsmen of the same workshop working side by side in the same villa.[30]

The list of examples already given of North African mosaics comparable with those of Piazza Armerina could be greatly extended: almost all the themes can be paralleled, sometimes closely, sometimes in more general terms, with the mosaic pavements of Tunisia and Algeria. There are obvious affinities, for example, between the animal heads (shown frontally) set within laurel wreaths (in the great peristyle at Piazza Armerina: plate 4) and a pair of mosaics from Thuburbo Maius which depict both whole animals and animal *protomai* shown in profile, also set within laurel wreaths. Again, the latter (plate 36) recalls the oval peristyle mosaic (41) at our villa, where, however, acanthus rather than laurel entwines the animals (plate 37).[31] The delightful but not especially

38. *Triconchos* mosaic, detail of a giant's head in the east apse

skilled mosaic of the children's circus with its bird-drawn chariots (33) is now paralleled by a rather later floor of identical theme at Carthage.[32] There are, however, two major floors at Piazza Armerina which are not so readily paralleled on the African continent, and for stylistic reasons one of them has been very widely claimed as the work of a different 'school'. The two in question are the Circus mosaic of the baths (8) and the Carnage of Hercules in the *triconchos* (46).

The overall design of the Circus mosaic is an ambitious one, with a complex series of groupings and daring perspective, but its execution is not equal to its conception (plate 8). The human figures are particularly squat and two-dimensional, with a minimum of internal shading to give any life or depth to the flesh, while some of the spectators at one end, and the bungled (but difficult) rendering of the chariot crash, are among the crudest mosaic work of the whole villa; the stocky ponies, too, lack the flowing verve of those on the two Hunt mosaics.[33] We can explain this less accomplished standard of workmanship in one of two ways. Either a separate workshop was called in to execute this floor – one perhaps which specialized in detailed circus scenes which the patron was anxious to have; or the most skilled and competent craftsmen were already fully engaged on other floors at the villa, with the result that only mosaicists of the second rank were deputed to work on the Circus

39. Mosaic in room 27, detail of the head of Polyphemus

mosaic. In view of the hypothetical links which can be established between the rest of the mosaics in the villa, it would not seem likely that this floor is the only odd one out; the alternative is therefore preferable. It is, nevertheless, surprising that a mosaic of this size and ambitious planning was not entrusted to more competent craftsmen. Perhaps the owner stipulated that the main living quarters, guest rooms and banquet rooms had top priority, and that the baths were to take second place; and in this connection it is worth noting that the whole *frigidarium* mosaic (9) is also of a standard far inferior to that of identical subjects elsewhere in the villa. It is an indication that the resources of the mosaic teams were being stretched to their utmost in the fulfilment of this contract for the *dominus*. At any rate the home of the Circus mosaicists is again likely to have been North Africa. Even though no good parallels exist there, Dunbabin has advanced hypothetical but convincing arguments for an African, and in all probability a Carthaginian, origin.[34]

With the mosaics of the great trilobed *triclinium*, however, we are very definitely dealing with another set of craftsmen at the opposite end of the spectrum of competence. One has only to compare the head of Ambrosia (plate 40) with that in the south apse of the Great Hunt corridor (plate 13), or the head of a giant (plate 38) with that of Polyphemus (plate 39), to realize that the mosaicists of the *triclinium*

40. *Triconchos* mosaic, head of Ambrosia in the south apse

41. *Triconchos* mosaic, detail, weeping horse

42. *Triconchos* mosaic, detail, another horse

had an understanding of figure drawing and a subtlety and variety in the use of polychromy quite unknown to the lesser craftsmen we have so far been considering. Furthermore the bold foreshortening of many of the figures and the detail paid to the anatomy indubitably place the artists who designed, and the craftsmen who executed, these mosaics at the very top of their craft. They also excelled in the depiction of suffering: we feel the agony of the giants in their writhing death throes, we feel the tears shed by the very human horse below the Hydra of Lerna (plate 41; cf. also plate 42). Where the mosaicists for these floors came from is less obvious, as there are few other mosaics to match their grand scale of conception. Carandini has pointed out some rather dubious African parallels, at the same time also admitting the possibility of an eastern mosaic school, but in a later study he opted for Mauretanian influence, although once again his parallels do not seem very convincing.[35] There has also been doubt about the date of these mosaics, which some scholars have claimed as being 'definitely of a later epoch' than those elsewhere in the villa.[36] Yet the cupid mosaics in the rooms flanking the adjacent elliptical court are, as we have seen (p. 39), clearly contemporary with the rest of the floors, and since these rooms and the court owe their very existence to what was clearly designed as a focal point at the east end, the *triconchos* was surely designed from the start as that focal point.[37] Nor is there any secure archaeological evidence which suggests

43. *Triconchos* mosaic, detail, the dying Marathonian bull

44. Mosaic in the corridor of the Great Hunt, the capture of the bull (detail)

45. *Triconchos* mosaic, south apse, detail of cupid

that even if the walls of the *triconchos* were built at the same time as the rest of the villa the mosaics themselves were not added until later.[38] Despite, however, very real differences in the scale of the figures and the more skilful and ambitious standard of the composition, detailed comparisons between some parts of the *triconchos* mosaic and others elsewhere in the villa reveal that the dissimilarities are not as striking as might first seem apparent. Some of the animals depicted in the Carnage, for example, are not all that markedly different from some of those in the Great Hunt (compare plates 43 and 44);[39] the gaily painted boat, duck and plants in a little known and very damaged part of the mosaic near the south-west corner immediately recall other such depictions at Piazza Armerina; and the splendid cupids in the Lycurgus and Ambrosia apse are recognizable, if much healthier and chubbier, brothers of the cupids elsewhere in the villa (compare plates 45 and 46). In fact these cupids share a feature in common with the other cupids and young boys at Piazza Armerina: they often bear a small v (or sometimes an x or a diamond) on their foreheads.[40] This is precisely the sort of idiosyncratic feature that one might expect to serve as a kind of trade-mark for one particular set of designers, and once again it is not without significance that the same oddity appears on some cupid mosaics at Carthage and occasionally elsewhere.[41] Until more material has come to light it is perhaps unwise to speculate further, but it would not be surprising if mosaics comparable to those in the Piazza Armerina *triconchos* were

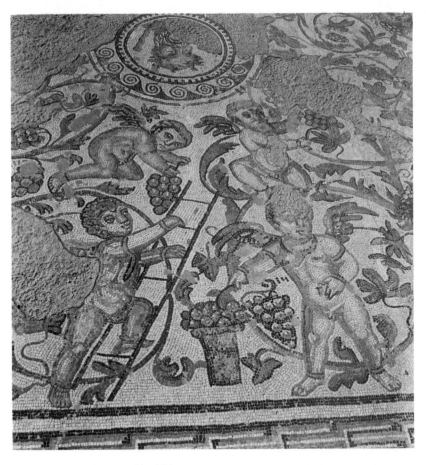

46. Mosaic in room 42, cupids picking grapes

one day discovered in the Carthage area of North Africa. At any rate it is by no means impossible that the mosaics of the *triconchos* were laid at precisely the same time and by precisely the same workshop as the rest.

The evidence is often tenuous and some of the threads may snap as more mosaic material accumulates in North Africa and elsewhere in the Roman world. But the tentative conclusion that seems to emerge is that there is at present no convincing argument against assigning all the Piazza Armerina mosaics to the same workshop, almost certainly one based at Carthage. The standard is not uniformly high throughout the villa – the level varies from the brilliance of the *triconchos* mosaics to the mediocrity of some parts of the floor showing boy musicians (34) or of that in the *frigidarium* – but these differences need not imply different workshops but rather differing levels of ability within the same workshop. And if it is right to suppose that only one *officina* was responsible for the whole of the Piazza Armerina compositions, then this reflects the enormous range of talents, presumably of scores of craftsmen, at the disposal of one single North African enterprise. The mosaic industry there on any account was big business; and given the insatiable appetite for mosaics that the town dwellers of Africa had – and the villa floors of the countryside there are as yet largely unknown – the existence of a single mosaic factory on this enormous scale is by no means to be discounted.

Chapter Three
Context and Ownership

So far our focus has been almost exclusively on the excavated structures at Piazza Armerina and on the glittering sumptuousness of its decoration. To set the villa in context against the broader background of late-Roman Sicily and the late-Roman world in general is a harder task beset with problems not easily resolved. In particular three major questions must be asked. First, do we know enough of the immediate surroundings of the villa to state confidently whether the excavated buildings are an isolated unit, the pleasure-palace of some rich man's whim, or whether it forms the centre of an active farming estate which provided the basis, at least in part, for the wealth which the villa so extravagantly displays? Secondly, is Piazza Armerina a unique phenomenon or can it be matched by villas of similar size or luxury elsewhere in Sicily, or indeed elsewhere in the Empire? And thirdly, a question closely related to the last, do we have enough evidence to suggest the social *milieu* to which the villa's owner belonged? Are we to think of a rich private individual, a member of the aristocratic senatorial class, or is it rather the property of the state, either for the use of some high-ranking imperial official, or even, as many scholars have cogently argued, for no less a person than the emperor himself?

Piazza Armerina and its immediate hinterland

The first of these questions cannot be settled without further excavation. We have noted earlier (p. 23) that the excavated buildings cannot have stood alone as no evidence of service quarters has so far been forthcoming. Some structures are visible in section in the earth bank immediately south of rooms 44–5, and tiles and other debris in orchards south-east of 46 suggest the presence there of further buildings, none of very great extent. The principal service quarters, however, most probably lie to the north of the villa on the uphill slope out of sight from the main residential block: numerous walls cut in section, as well as fallen roof debris, are visible in the exposed section of earth bank which marks the limit of the work carried out in 1950–4. This is particularly clear immediately north and north-east of room 17A, and more structures are visible for some 40 m along the cut running parallel to the aqueduct. The date of these structures is not immediately apparent. It is possible that they belong to the Byzantine or later periods when the villa was no longer functioning as the residence of a great owner,[1] but the position of room 17A, with its exterior doorway, does strongly suggest that there were service quarters contemporary with the villa on this side, and that servants entered the main residential block through this room. A large oven with blackened flue and flagged floor, still visible in the angle between 17A and 20, might support this hypothesis, but the structure is not mentioned in any published report and it is therefore uncertain if it is contemporary with the villa; it may well be later. Also visible at the site, but not *in situ*, is part of a lava mill for grinding corn into flour, and several storage jars *(dolia)*, both whole and fragmentary.[2]

That further buildings existed around the excavated villa is, therefore, indubitably clear. What is not clear is whether they comprised only a service block for the main residential quarters or whether they included agricultural buildings connected with farming an adjacent estate. By far the most usual way to obtain wealth in the Roman world, as indeed in nearly all economic systems before the Industrial Revolution, was from the land, and it remains at least a strong possibility that the *dominus* of Piazza Armerina also owned considerable tracts of farming land in the vicinity of the villa, especially to the south. Definite proof, however, is lacking; and this represents one of the most crucial deficiencies in our present knowledge about the site. Unfortunately too little detailed topographical work has yet been done in the region of Piazza Armerina to enable us to fit the villa into the wider settlement pattern of this area of Sicily in late-Roman times. The principal nucleus of habitation, as mentioned above (p. 13), lay 6 km south of the villa amid rolling arable land (see plate 47). This was the settlement of Philosophiana, listed in the road handbook known as the Antonine Itinerary as a *statio* on the Roman trunk route between Agrigento and Catania; and the identification, strongly suggested by the modern *contrada* name Sofiana, has been confirmed by the finding of a roof tile stamped FIL SOF.[3] Excavation here has uncovered a large bath-building dated to the early fourth century, as well as a church belonging to the fourth to sixth centuries. The settlement, which covered about 15 hectares, is ringed by cemeteries which have produced finds from the first century AD to Byzantine times, and the wealth of at least some of the inhabitants of what was predominantly no doubt an agricultural community is indicated by such outstanding finds as a pair of gold earrings of *c.* 500–600 with filigree decoration.

Further fieldwork around this settlement is badly needed. A few

47. Map showing the position of the villa in relation to other Roman settlement in the area (labelled in large capitals) as well as to modern roads and towns (S. Cono, Piazza Armerina; shaded). The necropolis immediately adjacent to the villa (p. 72) is not shown. The inset indicates the position within Sicily of the area covered by the main map, as well as the locations of the Roman villas of Patti and on the Tellaro discussed on pp. 73–7.

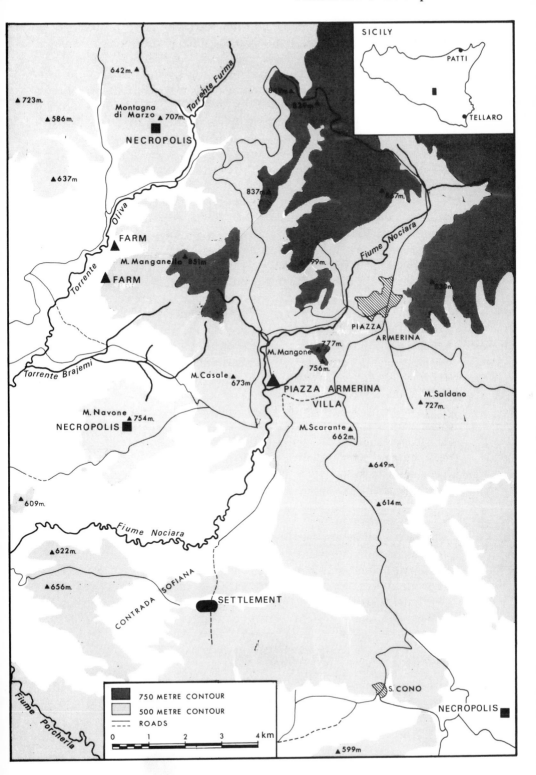

SICILY

PATTI

TELLARO

▲723m.

642m. ▲

Montagna
di Marzo ▲707m.
■
NECROPOLIS

▲586m.

Torrente Furma

▲637m.

837m▲

867m.

Oliva

Torrente

FARM ▲

M. Manganella ▲851m.

FARM ▲

Fiume Nociara

▲599m.

839m.

Torrente Brajemi

M. Casale ▲
673m.

M. Mangone ▲

777m.

756m.

PIAZZA
ARMERINA

PIAZZA ARMERINA
VILLA

M. Saldano
▲727m.

M. Navone ▲754m.
NECROPOLIS ■

M. Scarante ▲
662m.

▲649m.

▲609m.

▲614m.

Fiume Nociara

▲622m.

CONTRADA SOFIANA

▲656m.

SETTLEMENT

Fiume Porcheria

S. CONO

NECROPOLIS ■

750 METRE CONTOUR
500 METRE CONTOUR
ROADS

0   1   2   3   4 km

▲599m.

tombs with Roman pottery in *contrada* Mola (S. Cono) indicate the presence of a village or villa about 10 km south-east of Sofiana, and a couple of farms have been identified between the Brajemi and Oliva rivers about 5 km north-west of our site.[4] The hill-top settlement of Montagna di Marzo, which has produced material from the sixth century BC down to the end of the first century AD when it was abandoned, was apparently reoccupied in Byzantine times, as tombs with fifth and sixth century AD finds have been excavated there; and there is Byzantine material, too, from Monte Navone.[5] Finally, on the slopes of Monte Mangone close to our villa a necropolis of about a hundred tombs was unfortunately rifled by illicit digging in the 1920s. This was very probably the burial ground of the family who owned the villa and of their retainers and slaves, and the dispersal of the objects found there is particularly regrettable. One find, however, was rescued, a unique flagon of African red slip ware with mould-made decoration, probably of the fifth century AD.[6]

These meagre scraps of information about ancient settlement in the area throw little light on the Piazza Armerina villa. But the close proximity of our site to the market settlement of Philosophiana, to which it was probably linked by a separate road,[7] is of some interest. It is well known from evidence elsewhere in the Empire that in the late-Roman world individual landowners sometimes possessed vast tracts of land which might include not only many farms but even whole villages, and that the name of such settlements often enshrined that of the owner in adjectival form (ending in -*anus*).[8] Thus, to take two other Sicilian examples recorded both on tile stamps and in the Antonine Itinerary, the *latifundia Calvisiana* will have originally been formed by one Calvisius, and the *latifundia Petiliana* by a certain Petilius.[9] Philosophiana is clearly of the same type, presumably incorporating the *cognomen* Philosophus, which suggests a man of freedman class and probably of Greek origin.[10] Such a man, at some unknown period in the early Empire, may have formed a large estate which included several farms and at least part of the village in *contrada* Sofiana within its confines; his name then became enshrined in both the estate and the village records. If this is so, did whoever owned the villa at Piazza Armerina in the fourth century also own the settlement of Sofiana and some of the neighbouring sites just mentioned, which may or may not have also belonged to the *latifundia Philosophiana*? Such a hypothesis has found favour with several scholars,[11] but all we can say at present is that there is not a single scrap of evidence which suggests any direct connection between the two sites. To assume, as some have done, that the owner of Piazza Armerina was this same Philosophus, and to speculate that this was a nickname ('the philosopher') indicating someone fond of his books, is entirely fanciful.

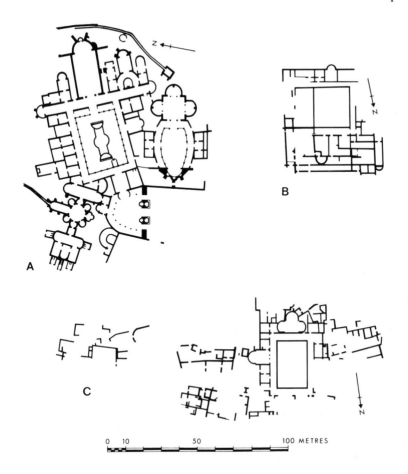

48. Plans of late Roman villas 1: Piazza Armerina (A), Tellaro (B), Patti Marina (C)

Piazza Armerina and other late-Roman villas in Sicily

Until comparatively recently Piazza Armerina remained the one late-Roman villa in the whole of Sicily of which the ground-plan was tolerably well known, and the absence of comparative material in the island only served to heighten the importance of the discovery. The existence of other villas of this date was indicated by several isolated bath-buildings, scattered finds of mosaic pavements and surface pottery sherds,[12] but in no case had systematic or extensive exploration been carried out.[13] In the last ten years, however, two discoveries of exceptional importance have helped to throw fresh light on the prosperous conditions of late-Roman Sicily, and to set the villa at Piazza Armerina more sharply in focus. The first site lies on the Tellaro river in south-east Sicily, about 5 km south of modern Noto (for the location, see inset of plate 47).[14] The villa, which so far has been only partly explored (see plate 48B), is situated on a slight rise overlooking a lush river valley surrounded by rich agricultural land consisting of arable interspersed with vines. Trenching has revealed that there were rooms on all four sides of a central peristyle 20 m square (that at Piazza Armerina measures 30 m by 25 m), with an apsed room of modest dimensions in the middle of the south side; but it is so far only on part of the north side of the peristyle, where excavation has reached floor levels, that the lavishness of the villa has been revealed. Both the corridor and three rooms opening off it are carpeted with splendid polychrome mosaics; that in the corridor has an intricate geometric design, but the rest are figured. One shows a mythological scene of Odysseus, Achilles and Diomedes (all identified by labelling in Greek letters) being begged by Priam to release the body of Hector. Another has an elaborate floral pattern woven round figured panels, one of which features a satyr and a maenad. But the outstanding floor from Tellaro so far, carpeting a room 6.40 m by 6.20 m, depicts a rich and lively series of hunting scenes (plate 49), many of which can be closely paralleled on the floors at Piazza Armerina: animals pounce on their hunters, while elsewhere the hunters are poised to strike; a leopard is lured into a baited cage; a wheeled ox-drawn waggon carrying shields is crossing a stream; and at the bottom of the tableau an open-air banquet is taking place under an awning slung between the trees. Dominating the centre of the composition is a much larger seated female figure who dwarfs the three officials in charge of operations standing alongside her. She is clearly a personification, possibly of Africa, the likeliest source of most of the animals shown in the mosaic.

Although many of these scenes bear a close resemblance in general terms to the Hunt mosaics at Piazza Armerina, and may well also be the work of imported African craftsmen,[15] the figure drawing in the Tellaro villa is more stylized, the men and animals more two-dimensional. The overall effect of a crammed and crowded tableau is also different from the schematic registers of the Small Hunt, or the fluid but still uncrowded composition of the Great Hunt at the Piazza Armerina villa. All this would suggest a later date for the Tellaro mosaics, and this is confirmed by numismatic evidence. The latest coin in a group of 108 found in the floor make-up in one room was an issue of AD 346, and another coin of the same period has been found under the Priam mosaic. The Tellaro villa, therefore, appears to have been built not earlier than the middle of the fourth century AD, although traces of an earlier structure, perhaps put up in the first century, have been found below, and second-century pottery lies on the surface outside the area so far explored.[16] Much more work clearly remains to be done here. Further mosaics will no doubt be discovered, and surface debris

49. Tellaro villa, hunting mosaic, detail

continues for at least 75 m north-west of the peristyle:[17] the villa is
clearly much larger than the 3,000 or so sq. m covered by the central
block which has been the focus of excavations so far.

Of even greater interest, if only because more of it has been explored,
is the very large Roman villa discovered on the north coast at Marina di
Patti during motorway construction work in 1973.[18] The motorway has
now been diverted and excavation is still proceeding at the site, but it is
already clear that the complex of buildings here covers an area of at
least 200 m by 100 m or 2 hectares (plate 48C). This is in fact larger than
the excavated building at Piazza Armerina (150 m by 100 m), but it must
be remembered that some of the structures at Patti Marina are
outbuildings, in part connected with agricultural production (an olive

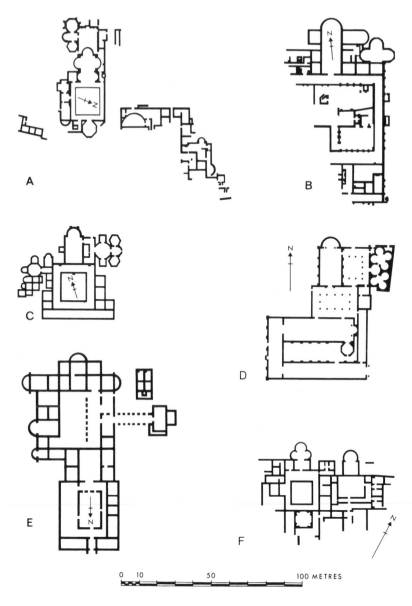

50. Plans of late Roman villas 2: Desenzano (A), Ravenna (B), Löffelbach (C),
     Gamzigrad (D), Fenékpuszta (E), Rioseco de Soria (F)

pipper has come from one room[19]), and that such outbuildings still await excavation at Piazza Armerina. The discovery of these outbuildings is in itself of great importance, because careful examination of them should reveal a great deal about the economic basis of this and similar villa-estates. The central, residential part of the villa, entered from the west, is arranged around a peristyle which boasts dimensions (27 m by 18 m) not far short of that at Piazza Armerina (30 m by 25 m). There is a large apsed salon in the middle of the east side but the main focal point, presumably the principal dining-room, is the distinctive three-apsed hall in the centre of the south wing. This of course immediately recalls the *triconchos* at Piazza Armerina, although the example at Patti is rather less imposing, measuring only about 16 m by 12 m (cf. 24 m by 19 m). The bath-suite has also been located, north-east of the peristyle and on a slightly different alignment. Several rooms in the villa are known from trial trenching to have had polychrome mosaic floors, but so far only those of the peristyle corridor have been extensively uncovered. The composition there is largely geometric, but animals adorn the circular medallions in the strip in front of the *triconchos*.

It is too early yet to be able to give a precise chronology for this great complex; but the excavator, Dr Voza, thinks that stylistically these mosaics fall within the fourth century, and the presence of the *triconchos* also squares well with a date not before *c.* 300. It was not, however, the earliest villa on the site, and excavation in the centre of the peristyle has revealed walling and geometric mosaics belonging to an earlier villa, probably of the second century, which was entirely razed to the ground when the fourth-century villa was built. The later history of the site is also of considerable interest. An earthquake caused the villa walls to collapse, but this occurred after the mansion had been abandoned and the roof had fallen in (the walls and their plaster had fallen over the collapsed roof debris). Burials made in and around the area of the baths produced gold jewellery and pottery of the sixth to seventh century, and crudely built structures criss-cross the site indicating continuing occupation on a more humble scale right down into Arab and early-medieval times. Even though the precise date of the abandonment of the villa as such, or of the subsequent collapse of the walls, has not yet been clarified, it is unlikely to have been later than the sixth century. This sequence of occupation bears a striking similarity to what we know about Piazza Armerina.

It is hard to overestimate the importance of these two discoveries for the understanding of Piazza Armerina and of late-Roman Sicily as a whole. No longer is Piazza Armerina an isolated phenomenon, as it can now be shown that large peristyle villas with lavish polychrome mosaic pavements existed elsewhere in Sicily during the fourth century AD. The two new villas appear not to show the same eccentricities of planning that Piazza Armerina does, and neither may quite rival Piazza Armerina either in size (allowing for unexcavated outbuildings at the latter) or in sumptuousness of decoration; but all three are clearly in the same class of luxury country dwelling of which no doubt many more examples await discovery in Sicily.

Piazza Armerina and villas elsewhere in the late-Roman world

But it is not only in Sicily that little research has been conducted on late-Roman villas: surprisingly few examples have been excavated anywhere in the central Mediterranean world. In particular it is extraordinary how little work has been done in the countryside of Roman North Africa: apart from a handful of *villae maritimae* of early or mid imperial date and the recovery of scattered mosaics elsewhere, virtually nothing is known about the physical appearance of country villas in North Africa, and the depictions of such buildings on the mosaics of town houses are at present our chief source of evidence.[20] Nevertheless there are some features of Piazza Armerina which suggest the possibility of influence from North Africa. Apart from being the homeland of the craftsmen who executed the mosaics, it is also not inconceivable that the architect of the villa hailed from there as well. The distinctive architectural creation of the *triconchos*, for example, appears to have its roots in the urban domestic architecture of late third-century North Africa;[21] the plan of central peristyle, long trans-verse corridor and large hall beyond finds a ready parallel in a late-Roman town house at Portus Magnus in Algeria; the horseshoe-shaped court with rooms opening off it (rooms 31–6 at Piazza Armerina) is a feature paralleled in Roman buildings in Tunisia; and the use of continuous rows of interlocking tubular tiles as a roofing material, which occurs only sporadically in Sicily, is a feature of specifically African derivation.[22] But it would be wrong to overestimate the extent of African influence at Piazza Armerina: the architecture of Roman North Africa was itself shaped at every turn by developments on the Italian mainland, and the Sicilian villa is essentially an example of the classical peristyle house which, while ultimately of Greek origin, first took on a more developed, elaborate form in mainland Italy.[23] The truth is that much more work is needed in the central Mediterranean before the precise architectural significance of Piazza Armerina can be appreciated within the wider context of late-Roman villa architecture. The bath-suite, for example, is of a type found frequently in North Africa in the third and fourth centuries, but it is a type ultimately inspired by the great imperial bath-buildings of Rome and which is seen reflected on a smaller scale in other examples in central Italy.[24] A major obstacle to fuller understanding of the architectural lineage of Piazza Armerina is

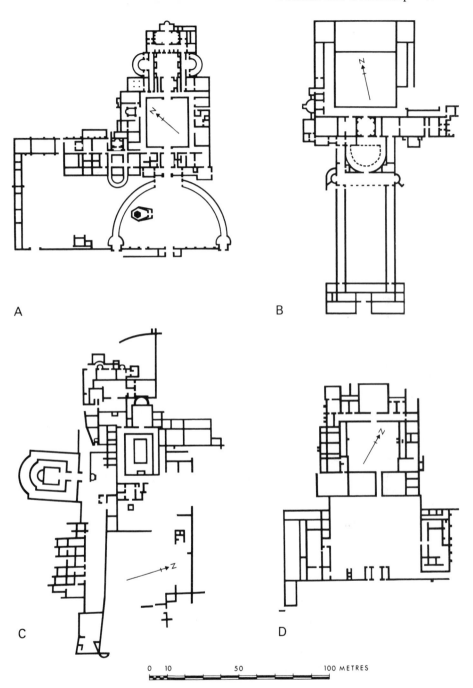

51. Plans of late Roman villas 3: Montmaurin (A), Valentine (B), Milreu (C),
Woodchester (D)

the dearth of extensive excavation in the late-Roman villas of southern Italy; such evidence as there is would imply that very large and well-appointed mansions were not lacking there either. At Casignana near Locri, for example, in the toe of Italy, excavation has uncovered part of the bath-suite and other rooms belonging to a Roman villa which in its visible form is probably to be dated between the mid third and the fourth century, and which was adorned with marble and figured polychrome floor mosaics (rather crude in execution) and frescoed walls. Yet this excavated portion is only a tiny part of what was clearly a very large and well-appointed villa, for surface finds and scattered fragments of standing walling elsewhere suggest a villa at least 200 m long and probably 100 m wide.[25] Fifth-century buildings at the rather smaller site of S. Giovanni di Ruoti near Potenza, currently under excavation, include an interesting apsed hall about 17 m by 8.50 m.[26]

Rather better known are two late-Roman buildings at the opposite end of Italy. The villa at Desenzano (plate 50A), on the shores of Lake Garda; offers us a splendid glimpse of a richly appointed fourth-century villa on the Italian mainland. Even though recovery of the complete plan is hampered by the presence of modern buildings, it is clear that the villa was grouped around several courts, with a playing fountain to the west and extensive baths to the north. What is of particular relevance to Piazza Armerina, however, apart from the presence of a three-apsed hall *(triconchos)*, is that nearly every one of the many rooms so far uncovered was floored with striking polychrome mosaics, several of them figured. Even the subject matter, and in particular the scene of fishing cupids in the *triconchos*, can be paralleled in the Sicilian villa and raises interesting questions as to the extent of influence that the African mosaicists enjoyed in mainland Italy.[27] The second building is a town house and not a villa, and is rather later in date: but the so-called 'Palace of Theodoric' at Ravenna, with its central peristyle, great apsed hall, and *triconchos* to one side, very clearly belongs to the same architectural family as Piazza Armerina (plate 50B).[28] The subject matter of the fragmentary mosaics there, which feature circus, amphitheatre and athletic scenes as well as a boar-hunt and other animal compositions, also recalls the Sicilian villa. Their precise date is uncertain. They probably belong to the late fourth or the first half of the fifth century, but not as late as the time of Theodoric (AD 493–526), with whom the building has sometimes been associated on insufficient evidence.

Nor are such mansions of elegance and sophistication confined to Italy or the central Mediterranean area alone. The letters of Sidonius Apollinaris make it clear that central southern Gaul in the fifth century AD was well stocked with comfortable country houses where members of the senatorial aristocracy, like himself, stayed during their long periods of *otium* – 'relaxation'. Sidonius has left us a vivid picture of his

52. Montmaurin, view from the inner court looking towards the entrance (right, background)

own favourite estate of Avitacum, near Clermont-Ferrand, with a portico overlooking a lake, main façades facing north and south, and a bath-suite on the south-west.[29] Sidonius never tells us the size of this villa but it is clear from his description that there were very many rooms.[30] Archaeological confirmation of such luxury dwellings in Gaul has also been forthcoming, especially from the area further south near the foothills of the Pyrenees. Two sites in particular are outstanding, both of them of a size which compares very favourably with Piazza Armerina. One is the splendid mansion of Montmaurin, which had been a house of notable size as early as the first century AD, but which was greatly enlarged and redesigned in its final form *c*. AD 330–50 on a most lavish and ambitious scale (plate 51A).[31] An entrance gate leads into a huge semicircular porticoed court, which in turn leads through a broad vestibule (cf. room 3 at Piazza Armerina) to the large peristyle around which the main living- and dining-rooms are arranged. The baths and charming interior courts are to be found to the west and south-west, and a further group of rooms and colonnades is set around an inner court on a higher level at the north end (plate 52). On an equally grand scale is the nearby villa of Valentine, also dated to the first half of the fourth century, but here agriculture has destroyed the walls to foundation level and removed many of the floors, and a canal has completely demolished the north wing of the mansion (plate 51B).[32] Here once again an entrance block leads into a huge courtyard, this time rectangular, at the far end of which is a transverse corridor with apsed ends reminiscent of the Great Hunt corridor in the Sicilian villa (plate 53). This in turn leads to a great ornamental D-shaped pool, beyond which the main living rooms are to be found, ranged around four sides of an inner court. At both Montmaurin and Valentine the local white marble from the quarries of St Béat was widely employed for columns, capitals and wall veneers; painted frescoes are also known at both: and at least a dozen rooms in each villa are known to have had polychrome geometric mosaics, although more may have once existed. At Valentine a detached bath-house found in the nineteenth century is known to the south-west of the main villa; also adorned with mosaics and marble, it was no doubt intended for the estate workers as well as for the owner, who may in any case have had his own suite in the villa proper. Later in the fourth century the villa at Valentine was almost certainly owned by one Nymphius, whose verse tombstone, even allowing for the adulation customary on such documents, gives us a valuable glimpse of his activities – as a member of the provincial council, as a donor of amphitheatre displays (*munera*), as a much-loved patron with a wide *clientela*.[33] All this provides striking confirmation of what can be gleaned from the literary evidence about the activities of rich villa-owners in the late Empire (see p. 94).

Other provinces as well have yielded examples of large and lavish late-Roman villas. Many are now known, for example, in the Iberian peninsula, although few there have been subjected to either complete excavation or to rigorous chronological examination: most villa-plans are incomplete and there are many uncertainties about date. That recently excavated at Rioseco de Soria, however, certainly belongs to the late third century (plate 50F): spaciously arranged around two peristyle courts, the villa boasts both a *triconchos* and an apsed hall (though of less imposing dimensions than at Piazza Armerina) and no less than 30 rooms with mosaic floors.[34] But neither Rioseco de Soria nor any other late-Roman villa in the Spanish provinces so far known, can compare in overall size with the vast villa at Milreu, on the Algarve coast of Portugal (plate 51C). Some details of this site, known and plundered since the seventeenth century, are only recorded from a survey made in 1877, but the main elements of a central peristyle with its garden pool, a large apsed hall beyond, and the spacious bath-suite on the south-west, are clear enough. This huge complex was probably also laid out in the late third century, although the imposing temple to the south was added in the first half of the fourth century. Many finds of marble sculpture have been made in this villa, and at least fourteen fragmentary geometric mosaics are recorded (apart from those in the temple), but more were probably plundered in the eighteenth and nineteenth centuries. Even distant Britain provides an example of a villa, substantially of fourth-century date in its known layout, which does not completely pale into insignificance beside Piazza Armerina: the country residence at Woodchester (plate 51D), explored by Lysons in 1793–6, had 15 mosaic-paved rooms grouped around the inner court, including the stupendous composition of Orpheus charming the birds and beasts which decorated a central salon 15 m square.[35] Frescoed walls and marble statuary and veneer are present here too; and it is clear from other discoveries from outside the area excavated by Lysons, including fragments of further mosaics, that the Woodchester villa extended over an area at least 180 m by 105 m.

The vast majority of late-Roman villas elsewhere in Britain and the northern provinces were, of course, on a much smaller scale; but even some of those, such as the peristyle villa at Löffelbach in Austria (plate 50C) with large apsed hall and striking variety of room shapes,[36] bear a superficial resemblance in general layout to the Piazza Armerina mansion. One group of villas in the Balkan provinces, however, deserves a brief review before we return once more to Sicily and focus our attention again on Piazza Armerina. In Pannonia and upper Moesia (the area which today includes parts of Austria, Hungary and Yugoslavia) a number of spacious peristyle houses in both town and country

53. Valentine, the corridor with apse and the columns lining the D-shaped pool, seen from the south-west

appear to have been newly built in the late third and fourth centuries, sometimes with large apsed halls as their principal rooms.[37] An earlier villa, at Pandorf in Austria, was also refurbished about the same time with a similar grand hall and fresh mosaic pavements in the larger rooms. Two sites, however, appear to be of particular significance. One is the double-courtyard building at Fenékpuszta in Hungary (plate 50E), a large but not luxurious structure of uncertain date, which, along with a granary, a church and several other outbuildings that look like the ancillary buildings of a farming estate,[38] were surrounded by immensely strong fortifications with gates and towers at some time in the late-Roman period. A very similar site appears to be Gamzigrad in eastern Yugoslavia, where an exceptionally large and luxuriously appointed mansion has been excavated in recent years.[39] The plan as so far uncovered is not readily paralleled elsewhere (plate 50D). In the centre is a long 'audience' hall, with an apse at its eastern end, and an octagonal room on its south side which has been interpreted as a robing chamber. This hall was approached along two spacious corridors from the main entrance at the south-east corner. North of the hall are two courtyards with marble colonnades, another large apsed hall presumed to be the dining-room, and a small bath-suite with rooms of trefoil and quatrefoil plan. It seems likely that the main living quarters of the building still lie buried immediately adjacent to the north-west. The floor mosaics in one room show hunting scenes which have been compared with those of the Great Hunt at Piazza Armerina,[40] and in the north hall, where the major portion of the floor is of marble *opus sectile*, a mosaic panel features Dionysus with a leopard. In addition the walls were decorated with frescoes and porphyry and other marble veneers, and the finds included luxurious stucco work and marble and porphyry statues. All the finds pointed to a date in the late third or early fourth century. This truly is a residence which rivals Piazza Armerina in magnificence.

Gamzigrad, like Fenékpuszta, was also surrounded by powerful walls. Several Roman emperors and their assistants (Caesars) are known to have had interests in the Balkans, and villas such as Pandorf have been claimed as the centres of imperial estates; but except for the palace of Mediana, a rich complex with mosaics and marble decoration which has also been explored in part, where the documentary evidence clearly indicates imperial ownership (Constantine may have been born there),[41] it is unwise to claim as 'imperial' any villa which happens to have more than a touch of luxury. While there are a number of villas in the Roman world, especially near the frontiers, which have defensive towers as an integral part of the villa-plan (such as Pfalzel in Germany), Gamzigrad and Fenékpuszta belong to a rather different and more exceptional class, in that they are surrounded by separate free-standing fortifications

54. Piazza Armerina, mosaic of the Great Hunt, the so-called *dominus*

in the manner of late-Roman forts or towns. It is most unlikely that a private individual would either have had the inclination or indeed have secured imperial permission to fortify a private estate in such an impressive way; and the presence of walls therefore strongly implies imperial ownership. In particular, the astonishing similarity in plan of the fortifications at Gamzigrad[42] to Diocletian's palace at Split, the presence of statues in porphyry, usually but not exclusively found at this date in an imperial context, and the fact that the province in which it lay (Dacia Ripensis) was the birthplace of the emperor Galerius, make extremely attractive the hypothesis that the luxury residence inside the walls at Gamzigrad was indeed designed by and for that emperor.[43]

Did an emperor own Piazza Armerina?

What emerges from this rapid survey of notable late-Roman villas elsewhere in the Empire is that Piazza Armerina is not entirely an isolated phenomenon but that it is still an exceptional building. Even though we must bear in mind that some of the plans in plates 50–1 include outbuildings as well as residential quarters, it seems clear that the size of Piazza Armerina is not unduly enormous. Large rooms for entertainment on an impressive scale are commonplace, and so too are buildings with a dozen or more mosaic-paved rooms. But the unortho-dox planning of the Sicilian villa, with its ever-shifting axes, does set it apart from the more formal arrangement of the rest of the buildings we have been considering; and even though all or nearly all of them are known to have been equipped with mosaics, marble and statuary, none of them quite rivals Piazza Armerina in the sumptuousness of its decoration: the Sicilian villa still remains head and shoulders above the rest as the most opulent country building yet known in the late-Roman world. Is it then the property of a private millionaire, or could it have been built by no less a person than an emperor?

The arguments for imperial ownership at Piazza Armerina have been strongly and persuasively put by several scholars, and the case must be now examined in some detail. In 1952 the Norwegian scholar H. P. L'Orange suggested that the villa was built by and for the emperor Maximian on his retirement from the purple in AD 305, a view which he further developed in a series of subsequent articles.[44] This theory was accepted by Gentili, the excavator of Piazza Armerina, after briefly entertaining a late-fourth-century date for the site.[45] The German scholar H. Kähler, after first supporting the Maximianic theory, subse-quently shifted his position and suggested that Maximian's son, Maxen-tius, was responsible for the complex, a view supported by Polzer and most recently by Settis.[46]

Their arguments are based partly on the architecture of the villa and partly on the subject matter of the mosaics. The mansion was designed, it is suggested, on a scale more suited to an emperor than to a private individual: in particular the monumental triple-arched entrance (plate 57) is reminiscent of an imperial triumphal arch, and the vast apsed hall (30) recalls the audience chambers of the imperial palaces in Rome and elsewhere where the emperor sat in judgment. The circular design in porphyry in the apse of the hall at Piazza Armerina is also interpreted as having exclusively imperial significance. The Proconnesian marble capitals used in the villa, furthermore, are reckoned by Kähler to resemble those of the emperor Diocletian's palace at Split in Yugoslavia so closely that both sets must have come from the same workshop at exactly the same time.

The argument based on the mosaics hinges largely on the occurrence

55. Mosaic of the Great Hunt, officials at the centre wearing flat-topped berets (detail)

on the Great Hunt floor of a distinctive cylindrical flat-topped beret, which is worn by at least two figures in the centre of the composition and also by the elderly man further to the right, the so-called *dominus* (master) (plates 54–5). A well-known porphyry sculpture group now at St Mark's, Venice, shows the co-emperors Diocletian and Maximian, together with their respective Caesars Galerius and Constantius (the Tetrarchs) all wearing precisely this headgear: it is, claims L'Orange, the 'incontrovertible argument for dating the mosaic to the era of the Tetrarchs' (i.e. 284–304).[47] For him the elderly figure on the Great Hunt (plate 54) was long to be identified as the emperor Maximian himself, but later he changed his mind and declared that the so-called *dominus* was only a magistrate, while Maximian was to be sought among the group of four figures ('the Tetrarchs') in the very centre of the Hunt corridor, at the foot of the steps to the audience hall.[48] The mosaic is damaged here, but Kähler has demonstrated that there is certainly room for only three, not four figures here; for him the central figure (left on plate 55) is the emperor Maxentius, for whom the villa was built, while the older official can indeed have been, as L'Orange originally proposed, Maxentius' father Maximian. If so, Kähler argues, the date of the Great Hunt can be pinpointed precisely: it must have been executed, he claims, after 306, when Maxentius became emperor, and before 308, when relations between father and son broke down completely; a portrait of his estranged father on a floor executed after this date would have been most unlikely. Among other people represented on the Piazza Armerina floors, the *domina* on the mosaic in the vestibule to the baths (plate 5) will, according to Kähler, have been Maxentius' wife Valeria Maximilla. She is known to have had two sons, who appear on the same mosaic; and as one of them, Romulus, died in 309, this floor must have been completed by that date.

Other features of the mosaics have been used to support the theory of imperial ownership. The fragmentary floor in 3, for example, has been interpreted as a welcoming ceremony (*adventus*) for an emperor (plate 56).[49] Hercules was adopted as the emblem (*signum*) of both Maximian and Maxentius, so that it is appropriate to find the outcome of their hero's labours depicted in the mosaics of the *triconchos*, including the glorification of Hercules in the north apse. A large head, probably from the statue which graced the apse of the 'Basilica', is variously interpreted as Hercules or as Maxentius depicted as the hero Hercules.[50] A fragmentary inscription has also been restored to support the Hercules interpretation, but this must be regarded as fanciful as only ten letters of it survived.[51] Gentili also argued that the ivy leaf, the *hedera*, was another motif of the family, its initial letter, H, also standing for Herculeius: hence its appearance on the shoulder-badge of the attendant to the left of the so-called *dominus* in the Great Hunt (plate 54) and in many other of the Piazza Armerina mosaics.[52] Finally, Settis has seen an elaborate symbolic significance in the subject matter of the mosaics. The Great Hunt shows imperial dominance of the world from east to west, he claims: it also symbolizes the amphitheatre, just as mosaics in the baths represent the Circus (8) and the stadium (11), the three places in Rome where the emperor's munificence could be displayed to his people. But the emperor, Settis goes on, is also master over the brute force of the passions (symbolized by Pan, Polyphemus and the animals) and triumphs over his enemies (the Giants, Lycurgus), thanks to his valour (*virtus*), protected by Hercules, and his good fortune (*felicitas*), protected by Bacchus. The one who best suits this billing is reckoned to be Maxentius who, it is alleged, had close connections with both Rome and Africa.[53]

Here then we have a set of arguments in favour of the theory that an emperor built and owned the Piazza Armerina villa. How conclusive are they? Certainly the chronology they imply – *c.* 305/6 to *c.* 310/12 – is not at variance with the archaeological evidence. Yet all the arguments presented above in favour of imperial ownership are also open to other interpretations; none is inconsistent with the possibility that the villa at Piazza Armerina belonged to a private, albeit very rich, individual.

Let us start with the Great Hunt figures wearing berets, important cornerstones in the theories of L'Orange and Kähler. Do they really bear the stamp of imperial personages? The headgear is indeed popular during the period of the Tetrarchy, although it is not exclusively worn by emperors: lesser officials, for example, wear it on the Arch of Galerius at Thessalonike. But it need not be exclusively of Tetrarchic date either: it is worn by soldiers on the Arch of Constantine in Rome, for example, in a scene carved perhaps *c.* 312/5, as well as on sarcophagi later in the fourth century, and on an ivory diptych in the fifth century.[54] Whatever the precise date, the personages on the Great Hunt, especially those in the centre of the floor, are directly involved with the capture and transport of the animals, an activity hardly becoming to an emperor but one which rather would have been supervised by lesser officials; if an emperor did own the villa, it is unlikely that his portrait is to be sought in any of them.[55] Of the figures with staffs (*baculi*) on this pavement, the graver countenance, the more richly embroidered clothing and greater care taken in general by the mosaicist over the figure which has been dubbed the *dominus* (plate 54), would indeed suggest that this is the man who owned the villa and commissioned the mosaic; but there seems nothing definitely 'imperial' about this figure.[56]

The ivy leaf (*hedera*) has also been claimed as a special emblem of the *gens Herculia* which both Maximian and Maxentius adopted; but if that were so, one would expect to find it decorating the shoulder badges on all the male attendants at Piazza Armerina, not merely on a couple. In fact the actual motifs employed to fill these oval panels on clothing all belong to the standard 'fill-in' repertoire of which mosaic borders and geometric floors are composed. It is, furthermore, an emblem more appropriate to Bacchus than to Hercules.[57] On the other hand the ivy leaf does appear in some rather odd places on the mosaics at Piazza Armerina, and with a frequency that does suggest a special significance. We know from mosaics in North Africa that the professionals engaged to do battle with wild animals in the arena (*venatores*) organized themselves into rival troupes (*sodalitates*), and that various lucky symbols, among them the *hedera*, were adopted by each. In view of the involvement which the owner of the villa surely had, on the evidence of the Great Hunt corridor, with the business of transporting animals for the amphitheatre (see p. 97), it is possible that the ivy leaf was the symbol of a particular *sodalitas* which he privately backed.[58] Similarly in the Circus he is likely to have been an enthusiastic supporter of the Green faction, as it is the charioteer of the Greens who triumphs in both the villa's circus mosaics.

The mosaics in the three-apsed hall with their Herculean theme similarly need have no imperial connotations. They may just as easily have been commissioned by a member of one of the leading aristocratic families of Rome, many of whom were firm adherents of the old paganism:[59] the absence of precise parallels for these mosaics need not be due to any special significance of the villa, but rather to our ignorance

56. Mosaic in room 3, *adventus* scene (detail)

of the tastes of comparable villa-owners in contemporary Italy. Likewise there is no convincing proof that the so-called *adventus* mosaic in room 3 honoured an emperor (plate 56). Some kind of religious ritual was undoubtedly depicted here, and the candle-bearing figures can be paralleled elsewhere in late-Roman art;[60] but the ceremony might have been a 'welcome home' scene for a grand but non-imperial owner, or even, more simply, a sacrifice to the household gods for the well-being of the mansion and its inhabitants.[61]

As for the Proconnesian marble column capitals, supposed to be of Tetrarchic date, they are simply not subject to the sort of very precise chronology that Kähler has worked out for them: another scholar, for example, has suggested that they include reused examples and range in date from the second century to the early fourth.[62] Yet even if Kähler is right and the capitals did all come from the same workshop as those at Split, there is no reason why the same workshop should not have supplied both an imperial and a private customer: identical capitals do not automatically entail identical and therefore imperial ownership for the two establishments. Similarly arguments that the circular design of porphyry in the apse of the 'Basilica' at Piazza Armerina, a modest slab one metre in diameter, can be interpreted exclusively in a context of imperial ownership, appear misguided. Porphyry was included in the embellishments of Sidonius' villa in southern Gaul and it has been found as flooring or wall veneer in other late-Roman buildings of non-imperial ownership;[63] and even if it was a statue of the emperor which graced the niche above, what more appropriate gesture of loyalty to the imperial throne than to place a statue in the principal room of one's mansion?

The great apsed hall itself has also been claimed to be exclusively of imperial significance, and it has been compared to the known imperial audience chambers on the Palatine in Rome, at Maxentius' villa on the via Appia, in the imperial palace at Trier and in Diocletian's retreat at Split.[64] But it is misleading to think that only emperors held 'audiences': the rich and powerful aristocratic classes of the late Empire had themselves wide and important *clientelae*, connections with local families and towns which were often handed down from generation to generation. When in residence the wealthy landowner was constantly approached for advice, for influence, for benefactions, and the distribution of such favours was an integral part of the role of the patron (*patronus*). It is striking how recurrent a feature is the large apsed room on the principal axis in the buildings discussed above – Ravenna, Milreu, Löffelbach, Pandorf and so on – and it is not surprising to find it at Piazza Armerina as well. Even though the hall at Piazza Armerina is larger and more ostentatious than usual, imperial overtones are not unavoidable: the even more lavishly decorated 'basilica' of Junius Bassus at Rome, built only slightly later than the Sicilian villa and with gaudy decoration in figured *opus sectile*, provides an excellent parallel in what was undoubtedly private property.[65]

The final argument put forward in favour of imperial ownership is the presence of the triple-arched entrance (plate 57). There are no close parallels for such an entrance in a private villa, but to deny such a possibility is to ignore the enormous gaps in our present knowledge of late-Roman country villas. At Montmaurin, to take one example, there is only a single gateway flanked by towers or porters' lodges which led into the great semicircular courtyard; but it seems only a natural step for a richer man, insisting on a greater display of wealth and self-importance, to provide himself with a more grandiose entrance, and if one arch was regarded as insufficient three was the obvious alternative. At Piazza Armerina this was no inflated, ponderous propaganda monument: it had instead the lighter touch of playing fountains adorned with mosaics.

A few final words on the hypothesis that Maximian or Maxentius owned Piazza Armerina, and then we must leave it. The villa is situated in the very heart of Sicily, close, it is true, to the road from Catania to Agrigento but still in a remote spot. Unlike Gamzigrad, set in an area with which several emperors are known to have had close contacts, there is nothing that we know about in the careers of any emperors of the right date that suggests strong links with Sicily or makes it likely that they owned a secluded retreat in the centre of the island. Maximian, for

57. The triple entrance gate to the villa, from the south-west

example, gives us little sign that he had a taste for the retirement his colleague Diocletian cherished at Split.[66] In November 306 he reappears on the political scene, defeats Severus at Ravenna, is in Gaul in 307, returns to Italy the next year and then goes back to Gaul. He turns up at Carnuntum on the Danube in 308, and then two years later he was captured by Constantine near Marseilles, whereupon he was killed or committed suicide. The only time for 'relaxation' (*otium*) was in 305–6, and those years were spent in Campania according to one ancient writer, in Lucania (central southern Italy) according to another.[67] Nobody mentions Sicily. Maxentius was equally involved in hectic activity during the six turbulent years between his assumption of the purple in 306 and his death in the Battle of the Milvian Bridge in 312. If the villa really was commissioned for either Maximian or Maxentius it is clear that neither could have spent much time there. And what are we to suppose happened after 312? Did the next emperor Constantine spend his vacations there?[68] Or do we have to conjecture that he gave it away to one of his supporters in return for loyal service?

Other candidates for ownership of Piazza Armerina

The hypothesis, then, that Piazza Armerina was designed as the retreat for an emperor during his period of *otium* in the island seems incapable of strict proof; but it is not the only hypothesis that has been put forward. It has also, for example, been suggested that the villa was the official base of one of the great administrators of the imperial government, probably the chief procurator or financial official in charge of imperial estates in Sicily (*rationalis rei privatae*).[69] This theory has recently been developed at length by Giacomo Manganaro in a fresh study of the fragmentary inscriptions found during the excavations. These include three dedications of the first to third centuries AD which contain titles of emperors; an inscription of which only two words survive, *triclinium* (dining-room) and what Manganaro interprets as *emporium* (depot or market centre); and a rather longer text mentioning a temple and honouring a citizen, a decree set up by a municipal town council (*ex decurionum decreto*, 'by decree of the councillors'), presumed by Manganaro to be that of the nearest known town, Enna. He therefore concludes that in the earlier imperial period, the date of these inscriptions, the villa preceding the visible building was surrounded by a village (*emporium*) which, because of the imperial dedications, must have been in imperial ownership; and that the wealth of the fourth-century villa was a reflection of 'the increasingly important role of the imperial bureaucracy' in the late Empire. Manganaro's thesis, however, rests on the slenderest of evidence. The reading *emporium* is itself extremely dubious,[70] and it seems unlikely that a separate collecting depot for corn existed here in the early Empire when the market settlement of Philosophiana was itself so near. The finding of inscriptions with imperial titles need itself cause little surprise, for major building slabs in town and country alike may include dedications to emperors even when in private ownership; and there is not a scrap of other evidence suggesting that Piazza Armerina lay on an imperial estate. Much more serious an objection is the certainty that most if not all of these inscriptions are re-used material, and so far from being relevant to the early history of the site, they may not even be of Sicilian provenance: we have discussed above the likelihood that re-used marble slabs (p. 32) and possibly capitals (p. 90), were imported from Italy for the building of the fourth-century villa. It seems, furthermore, inherently unlikely that the villa was created by central government as the residence of a faceless bureaucrat; it has rather an intensely personal touch, reflecting the specific tastes of an individual *patronus* who commissioned the villa with an eye to permanent or semi-permanent residence.[71] In particular, the subject matter of the mosaics, with the possible exception of the Great Hunt corridor,[72] appears totally inappropriate to an imperial administrator. The operations of such officials are in any case more likely to have been conducted from the towns, presumably with a headquarters at the provincial capital, Syracuse, and the notion of an 'official' country seat where a governor or top administrator could spend his holidays is completely absent in antiquity: if a government official wanted a country mansion, then he had to buy it from his own purse.[73] Thus while some of the buildings on imperial estates must have been well appointed, especially if there was a chance of a visit or two from the emperor himself, the most sumptuous villas in Sicily are more likely to have been privately owned.[74]

That the size and luxury of Piazza Armerina are by no means incompatible with the living standards of the very rich senatorial class of late antiquity is abundantly clear from the literary evidence. We have already heard something of the life-style of these people in connection with Nymphius and Sidonius Apollinaris in fourth- and fifth-century Gaul, and many other glimpses can be obtained from the pages of Ammianus Marcellinus, Symmachus and others. The picture that emerges from the literary evidence is a striking one: the rich senator given over to a life of ease and luxury, spent in going to dinner parties and in hunting and in travelling from estate to estate, a life burdened only by the periodic interruptions of one-year magistracies, each interspersed by a decade or so of *otium*. For many of the senatorial class this was a sober and dignified existence, for others it was an excuse for over-indulgence, in food, in gambling, in entertainments, in ostentatious living as a whole. It is clear, too, that the wealth of these men was phenomenal as the incomes they amassed from their landed estates were vast.[75] The fact that Gamzigrad, where the case for imperial ownership is strong, happens to be the only country building of the same date which closely rivals Piazza Armerina in its degree of opulence does not in itself imply imperial ownership as well for the Sicilian villa: it is misleading to draw too sharp a distinction between the living standards of the imperial court on the one hand and those of the very rich senatorial class on the other. Similarly, there is nothing in the subject matter of the mosaics at Piazza Armerina which is not entirely consistent with what we know of the interests and activities of these private senators. Ammianus, for example, comments on their interest in charioteers and dancing girls, which calls to mind the Circus mosaics and, perhaps, the bikini-clad maidens.[76] Symmachus, himself the owner of three houses in Rome and its environs, and of no less than fifteen country residences elsewhere in Italy, scoured many parts of the Empire in assembling a rich assortment of animals which he and his son needed when presenting magnificent games to the people of Rome.[77] This clearly was also an activity close to the heart of the owner of Piazza Armerina (p. 97).

Private property-magnates active in Sicily are most likely to have belonged to one of two categories. The first is the Sicilian-born landowner. Few of the Sicilian aristocracy at any time during the Empire are known to have embarked on a senatorial career in the civil service:[78] they seem rather to have remained in Sicily, drawing their income from their country estates, but preferring, perhaps, for the most part to live in the towns. Their presence there during the period of the middle Empire is documented by such evidence as the mosaics of town houses at Agrigento, Marsala, Palermo, Syracuse and elsewhere, and by the great numbers of expensive, carved third-century sarcophagi. In the fourth century and later this urban-based aristocracy tended to settle more permanently on their country estates, a social phenomenon widely attested elsewhere in the Roman world.[79] This change in residence pattern, partly engendered by a desire for tax evasion, must have had a depressing effect on the morale of the towns: the emigration of the wealthiest urban gentry led in turn to an emigration of members of the artisan class who, faced with a less secure livelihood in the towns with the loss of their richest patrons, were forced to find a new life in the country either as tenant farmers or as craftsmen on one of the great estates. This explains both why the towns of Sicily, except for the largest, declined in the later Roman period, and why the villas of the countryside reached a new standard of lavishness with their mosaics and bath-houses, as well as a whole range of outbuildings for the estate retainers. The increasing self-sufficiency of the private estates, surrounded by outlying farms, villages and market-centres, is well attested elsewhere at this period,[80] although, as we have seen, at Piazza Armerina a large question mark still hovers about the existence of farm buildings at the villa and the nature of the surrounding estate. The Patti villa (pp. 75–7), apparently complete with outbuildings, provides an example of the phenomenon, and it is feasible that its owner was a rich Sicilian aristocrat who may have previously divided his time between a town house in a place like nearby Tindari and a modest but well-equipped country villa, but who now chose, at some stage in the fourth century, to transfer his entire wealth to the country and to construct a new and even more lavish establishment.

It is indeed possible that the owner of Piazza Armerina was himself a member of this Sicilian aristocracy; but it is perhaps more likely that he belonged to the other category of property magnate known to have been operating in Sicily, the Italian aristocracy. The island had attracted Italian property speculators from the time of the Roman Republic onwards, and Augustus gave leave to senators to travel to the province without requiring his specific permission, a concession which applied to only one other province, Narbonensis (southern France).[81] But while many Italian families may for generations have owned land in Sicily, one wonders how often they took the opportunity of visiting their estates there. In the late Empire this situation may have changed. In particular the increasing insecurity of central and northern Italy during late antiquity must have encouraged more and more Italians to migrate

58. Mosaic of the Great Hunt, gazelle, bull, rhinoceros and hippopotamus

southwards to the peaceful havens of south Italy and Sicily, and to equip their estates there with all the luxuries of their town houses in Rome. The process is, however, rarely supported by precise documentation. An imperial edict of AD 410 implies that many Italians took refuge in southern Italy and Sicily when the Visigoths were ravaging Italy,[82] and one of these was Melania who travelled southwards before the barbarian advance selling off her estates one by one. Some of these were enormously large, the size of small towns according to her biographer, with baths, workshops and quarters for agricultural workers.[83] For a time she took up residence on her Sicilian property where she and her husband Valerius Pinianus gathered around them a circle of friends to discuss religion and philosophy.[84]

Melania is an excellent example of the sort of wealthy leisured aristocrat to which the villa of Piazza Armerina may well have belonged, but her Sicilian estate lay somewhere near Messina, and her name has not been linked with Piazza Armerina; she lived, moreover, a century after our villa was built. Another well-documented Italian aristocratic family with strong Sicilian connections were the Nicomachi Flaviani. Nicomachus Iulianus, commemorated on an inscription of the third century by his estate manager near Erice in western Sicily, was probably of the same *gens*.[85] Then sometime around the middle of the fourth century we find Volusius Venustus as governor of Sicily, a post also held by his son Virius Nicomachus Flavianus in 364/5, and finally there is Venustus' grandson, Nicomachus Flavianus junior, who finished revising a text of Livy on his estate 'near Enna' sometime after 408.[86] Some scholars[87] have pressed the claims of the Flaviani, undoubtedly one of the last great pagan aristocratic families of Rome, immensely rich and powerful, as owners of the Piazza Armerina mansion; yet the pointer 'near Enna' (*apud Hennam*) is too vague for us to be able to connect the family convincingly with our site, which today is over 50 km by road from Enna. Nor is there any evidence to support another hypothesis that Claudius Mamertinus, prefect of Italy, Illyricum and Africa between 361 and 365, had anything to do with Piazza Armerina.[88] The only known connection he had with Sicily was his presence in Syracuse in February 362 when he was organizing troop movements in the island in preparation for a planned invasion of Africa which never materialized.[89] There is not a scrap of evidence that a man actively dashing around the Empire on various military enterprises ever owned a quiet and luxurious retreat in the remote heart of Sicily. Two other names that have been connected with the villa are again supported by insufficient evidence: Anicius Petronius Probus (consul in 406) on the basis of a fragmentary inscription found at Piazza Armerina;[90] and Sabucius Pinianus, possibly the Pinianus who was Urban prefect in 387, on the basis of a modern farm called Casale Sabuci about 6 km from the site.[91]

The evidence, then, that we have at present is not conclusive enough to give a name to the man responsible for building the villa now visible at Piazza Armerina. But while his identity still eludes us some of his interests and passions are spelt out for us in the subjects he chose for his mosaic floors. In particular it seems highly probable that he had more than Symmachus' passing interest in rounding up exotic animals: he may himself have been directly involved in what must have been the enormously complex and costly business of capturing and shipping these beasts to the amphitheatres that required them.[92] The clue, as already noted above, comes of course from the Great Hunt corridor, an architectural feature which must have lain at the very heart of the owner's plans for his country mansion, and which must have been on the architect's drawing board from the start. The explicit and detailed renderings on the mosaic here of the capture of beasts from many regions of the Roman world (plate 58) and of their transportation by sea does not smack of make-believe;[93] the interest in animals is further emphasized by the prominence given to them in the corridor mosaics of the two peristyles. Since mosaic pavements at this period do directly reflect the interests and activities of the patrons who commissioned them,[94] it seems very likely that the owner of Piazza Armerina had indeed made a fortune in the animal trade. The contacts that he must have had in North Africa, one of his principal sources of supply, will have stood him in good stead, no doubt, when he came to employ squads of mosaicists, and possibly even an architect, from that continent.

The owner of Piazza Armerina was, therefore, very probably a private individual of senatorial class, possibly a Sicilian, but more likely a member of one of the great aristocratic families of Rome. Like other men in this class he may well have held the occasional magistracy in Rome without being bent on an active political career. The Circus mosaic, for example, might well have been intended as a reminder of the lavish games that he had provided, as magistrate, for the enjoyment of the people of Rome (plate 59). He may also have conceivably been governor of Sicily at some stage in his career, like others of the senatorial class known to have owned property in the island,[95] but in no sense was this his official residence. Certainly he must have been a millionaire, one of the richest men in the Empire, wealthier than those who built the villas at Patti and on the Tellaro elsewhere in Sicily. For a very rich man who had amassed a fortune in the animal business to supplement no doubt a regular income from the rents and agricultural produce of other properties that he owned (and possibly from this villa as well), the mosaics would have been a constant reminder to himself and to his *clientela* of a successful career, as well as to his descendants who presumably inherited the villa on his death. To judge from the

59. Mosaic of the Circus, detail of the victorious charioteer

mosaics he was an unashamed hedonist, hunting being a favourite pastime, and his beliefs were firmly rooted in the old pagan religion and values, readily summed up by the exploits of the hero Hercules. Further than that one cannot safely go. For the moment he must stay anonymous; but the hope remains that his identity might one day be revealed by further work at Piazza Armerina, and that the Sicilian villa be matched by the discovery of other private country mansions of equal architectural and artistic magnificence.

Notes and References

Chapter 1

1. Antonine Itinerary 88.2 and 94.5; Adamesteanu 1955 and 1963.
2. Diodorus IV 84.1.
3. Especially the apsed wall at the rear of the oval court (41, see plate 1), the right pier of the entrance arch (1) and the apse of the 'Basilica' (30).
4. Leanti 1761, 144. For a fuller account of the early discoveries, Gentili 1950, 293–5; 1959, 9; 1966, 15–16; and Kähler 1973, 12–13.
5. Agnello 1965.
6. Orsi 1931.
7. Cultrera 1940.
8. Books: Gentili 1959, 1962, 1966; other major articles include Gentili 1952 a and b, 1956, 1957, 1958.
9. Gentili 1950: some of the lamps were also published separately, Gentili 1952 c. Cf. also the pottery lists of Gentili's finds published by Carandini in Ampolo et al. 1971, 203–6.
10. Ampolo et al. 1971.
11. Bernabò Brea 1947.
12. The walls survive high enough between 37 and 39 to be certain that this gap never contained a staircase (there are no doorways here).
13. The third and smallest latrine at Piazza Armerina, a detached, octagonal structure (47), was probably also intended for servants and estate workers, although it could be reached from the Hunt corridor (26) through the narrow alley between 30 and 35–6 (for Kähler 1973, 16, this is the children's toilet). The latrine, with a seating capacity of about five, has a floor mosaic (white ivy tendril springing from a bowl, on a black ground) and a wash basin.
14. For a detailed analysis of this, Gentili 1957.
15. The mosaic is clearly meant to represent three stages in any race, not three stages of the same race, as the horses' headgear and the charioteers' attire differ in each representation.
16. Terracotta tubes also appear with lava and pumice in the *tepidarium* vault, but these appear to be used only as *caementa*, i.e. a light constituent for the concrete mix. Gentili 1956 also speaks of terracotta tubes being found 'on top of the mosaics' but it is not clear how many rooms were roofed in this fashion; the apse of the 'Basilica' (30) was certainly one (Gentili 1966, 37). For the use of interlocking tubular tiles elsewhere in Sicily, Wilson 1979, 32. Cf. also Lugli 1963, 39, fig. 15. The *lampadedromia* mosaic is discussed in detail by Gentili 1975–6.
17. *Pace* Kähler 1973, 15 and Settis 1975, 924.
18. All the animals in the right-hand portion of the mosaic which are not found in more than one continent (i.e. in both Africa and Asia) come from eastern regions, e.g. the hippopotamus (Egypt), rhinoceros (India), tigress (Armenia or India), the mythical phoenix in the apse (Arabia, India or Ethiopia). Those in the left-hand portion are found more widely; but North Africa and the west in general is not an impossible source for all of them. The flaw in this argument is the presence of the elephant of African, not Indian species in the right-hand part of the mosaic and in the right apse. If the composition is consistent, and the identification of the south apse as the East is correct, then either the principal

source of elephants as envisaged by this mosaic was Ethiopia (where the African elephant was found in antiquity), or else the African-based mosaicist did not appreciate the difference between the species and drew the African variety when his patron intended the Indian (perhaps his copybook did not indicate both types). The earlier identification of the figure in the south apse as Africa (e.g. Gentili 1959, 22) cannot be correct: personifications of Africa in antiquity are never shown as dark-skinned, and neither tigress nor phoenix is associated with that continent (except for the latter in Egypt: Pliny *Natural History*, X.3). Carandini 1971, 131, favours Egypt (the alternative identification put forward by Gentili, ibid.): he thinks that the elephant might have come from deepest Egypt (Aegyptus Herculia), but his explanation that the presence of the tigress is logical because such animals would have embarked for Italy from Alexandria is unsatisfactory; if Egypt was intended we might have expected a hippopotamus or some other creature more readily associated with there. Nor, *pace* Picard 1978, can the figure be Ethiopia; even if the elephant (see above) and the phoenix (van den Broek 1972, 305–7) can be linked with that region, the tiger certainly cannot (Picard 1978, 27, note 8, suggests weakly that the tiger and the leopard may have been confused in antiquity). Picard also entertains the possibility, on the basis of a hoard of 38 Roman coins found in 1974 in the Ivory Coast, that west Africa *south* of the Sahara may have been a source of supply for some of the beasts (e.g. elephants) in antiquity: but there is not a hint of this in the ancient literature. For further discussion of the figure in the south apse, see L'Orange 1965, 93, Settis Frugoni 1975, 22, and Marrou 1978, 284–5.

19. For a detailed analysis of its composition, Carandini 1971. A classic survey of Roman hunting mosaics in general is Lavin 1963; cf. more superficially Hervel 1970. The hunting mosaics of Piazza Armerina are the subject of separate monographs by Gentili (1962) and Daltrop (1969).

20. Not commented on by Gentili 1959, 27–8 or by Renard 1960, who studies the theme in Roman art as a whole and suggests that it symbolizes the forces of good (*virtus*) over evil and the power of nature. The opinion of Cagiano de Azevedo (1967–8, 144) that the mosaic betrays the owner's interest in neoplatonism is entirely without foundation.

21. Kähler's (1973, 15–16) interpretation of rooms 31–6 as the *Kindervilla* (children's quarters) because of the subject of the mosaics there is untenable: he allots less space to the master and his wife (27–9). Cf. the refutation by Settis 1975, 941. Kähler's interpretation of the function of some of the other rooms is also open to serious doubt; for example he allots no less than seven rooms (18, 19, 21, 24, 25, 38, 39) to servants, as though no servants' quarters existed elsewhere (see p. 69)! For the kind of room-types that one might expect to find in a late-Roman country mansion, cf. Sidonius' description of his own villa at Avitacum (see note 30 of ch. 3).

22. Barreca, Sicari and Cremona 1967; cf. also Gentili 1959, 52–6.

23. E.g. a yellow breccia from Tripolitania (western Libya), eastern *lumachella* from Thuburbo Maius (Tunisia), *settebassi* from Scyros (Greece), and three marbles from Sibillius, Ezine and Caria (Asia Minor). There is also a *lumachella pavonazza* from either Gaul or Pannonia and a *breccia pavonazza sfangiata* of unknown provenance. See Ampolo et al. 1971, 221–3, and for a description and colour illustrations of many of the marbles listed, Gnoli 1971, passim.

24. There are other substantial traces of frescoes, especially in rooms 37 and 38: Gentili 1950, 322–4.

25. The best preserved is on the exterior of the apse of room 5, where the design consists of large solid circles in maroon with a 'toothed' edge of black triangles, and an imitation marble ('fried egg') pattern in red and yellow.

26. Pace 1955a, 105.
27. Cagiano de Azevedo 1961, esp. 26; on the dissimilarities, see especially L'Orange 1965, 89–90.
28. Carandini 1964, passim but especially 65–70.
29. Ragona 1966; Ammianus Marcellinus XVII.4.15.
30. Isidore, *Etym.* XVIII.31.2; for the Lateran circus relief, *Jahrbuch des Deutschen Archäologischen Instituts* lv (1940), 12.
31. Nash 1962, 137; for the dating, Ammianus *ad loc. cit.* in n. 29.
32. These arguments are also discussed by Carandini 1964, 39–40, L'Orange 1965, 90–2 and Polzer 1973, 149–50. Cagiano de Azevedo 1961, 26, accepted the off-centre position as a firm *terminus post quem* of 326 for the villa, but believed the omission of the 357 obelisk (surely the more significant point) as due to 'artistic licence'. More sensibly Lugli 1963, 67–8, takes the absence of a second obelisk as a *terminus ante quem* of 357 for the villa.
33. Gentili 1959, 74; cf. also his letter published in Picard and Stern 1965, 314.
34. Ampolo et al. 1971, 153–202.
35. Hayes 1972, 218–9, 291.
36. Lugli 1963, 78–80.
37. Kähler 1969, 42, and 1973, 19.
38. For some general comments on the architectural layout, in addition to works cited in notes 36–7, see especially Neuerburg 1959, Boethius and Ward-Perkins 1970, 529–32, and Di Vita 1972–3.
39. So Lugli 1963, 59; Kähler 1969, 45; 1973, 19; Bovini 1970, 37 and 52; Dorigo 1971, 150–1; on the other hand others, e.g. Pace 1955a, 96, and Dunbabin 1978, 200 (heavily qualified in n.16), think that stylistically the mosaics in the *triconchos* ought to be earlier rather than later than those elsewhere in the villa.
40. Excavation in area 40 has revealed earlier walls, but they belong to the pre-fourth-century villa and were demolished before the peristyle was built: Lugli 1963, 60–2 with fig. 15.
41. There is nothing in the pottery lists in Ampolo et al. 1971, 205–6, where the 1951 finds from under the floor and mosaic of the south apse of the *triconchos* are recorded, which hints at a *terminus ante quem non* other than the late third century, except for two pieces of Hayes 91 (Lamboglia 38), not earlier than the mid fifth century. If these have been correctly identified they must surely be intrusive material, as no scholar has suggested that mosaics or *triconchos* could be as late as the mid fifth century.
42. E.g. in the *frigidarium* of the baths (Gentili 1966, 21), in the apse of 39 (Kähler 1973, pl. 56b), at the left-hand end of 31.
43. Carandini 1971, 126 and figs 3–6.
44. Ampolo et al. 1971, 239, 250–1; cf. Gentili 1952a, 34 with n.12; 1959, 33. Lugli 1963, 47, wrongly thinks it is contemporary with the rest of the mosaics.
45. I here accept the interpretation of Traversari 1960, 75–83, followed by Marrou 1978, 285–95, rather than that of Pace 1955b, who imagined that the girls were engaged in water-sports (on the evidence of the blue band on which the action is taking place; but if so the mosaicist was surely competent enough to have depicted the girls ankle- or knee-deep in water). Certainly the spectacle was not designed to take place in the villa itself, as Lugli 1963, 52, would have us believe.
46. Gentili 1959, 33, 50–2 (Constantinian, *c.* 320–30), cf. Carandini 1964, 25–7 (second half of the fourth century).
47. The furnaces of the baths also show clear evidence of extensions and alterations (plate 9).
48. Di Vita 1972–3, 256–7; it is plausible to place the destruction of the baths at

Sofiana and their conversion to industrial use to this period (G. Manganaro, *Kokalos* xviii-xix (1972–3), 262).

49. This account is mainly based on scraps of information culled from Gentili 1966 and 1950, esp. 313–4, 334–5; cf. also Cagiano de Azevedo 1966, 672–3. Photographs of Byzantine and Arab pottery appear in Gentili 1950, 331–4, figs 32–4; cf. Ampolo et al. 1971, 261–81 at greater length. Removal of the 'Byzantine' structures in 41 is recorded by Bernabò Brea 1947, 253.

50. For burnt layers in 26 and 39, Gentili 1950, 314 and 325. But the rubbish layers presumably protected the mosaics there, and signs of burning on other mosaics (e.g. north-east corner of room 33, and behind the maenads of the south apse of 46) are few.

Chapter 2

1. Especially Carandini 1964, 43–65; Carandini 1967, 105–8; L'Orange 1965, 66–79 and Gentili 1959, passim. For a summary see now Dunbabin 1978, 196–201.

2. Gentili 1959, 11.

3. Dorigo 1971, 127–68.

4. Carandini 1971; see also the review of Dorigo's book (the 1966 Italian edition) by R. Bianchi Bandinelli in *Dialoghi di Archeologia* i (1967), 248–62.

5. Inscriptions on mosaics elsewhere seem to indicate that, at least sometimes, the designer (*pictor*) was distinct from the man who actually laid the pavement (*tessellavit* or *pavimentavit*): Dunbabin 1978, 27–9.

6. The point has also been made by Di Vita 1972–3, 257–8.

7. Dunbabin 46–64, and see note 19 of ch. 1.

8. Gentili 1959, 33–4.

9. Cagiano de Azevedo 1967–8, 144–9.

10. Dorigo 1971, 153.

11. ibid. 157.

12. Cf. the remarks of Dunbabin 1978, 53–4.

13. Only one example is known in North Africa: Dunbabin 1978, 29. For a recent discovery in France, Fouet 1979, fig. 4.

14. This is especially clear in some of the lesser floors: for example the standard of the figure drawing of Pan and Eros in room 35 is markedly superior to that of the spectators in the same composition.

15. For various attempts at estimating how work on the Great Hunt mosaic was divided up, see Gentili 1959, 11 (six groups of four workmen each) and Carandini 1971; and more generally on this problem, Gentili 1959, 44–9.

16. Pace 1955a, 108 note 1. For another estimate Dorigo 1971, 131 note 12 (a decade for the floors, but including wall and ceiling decoration, and interruptions, 25 years in all). Gentili, L'Orange and Kähler are forced for other reasons (see pp. 86–9) to assume that the mansion was substantially complete in about five years, and most or all of the mosaics laid.

17. Wilson 1982, 426–7.

18. A comparable project is the twelfth-century wall and vault mosaic work of the cathedral at Monreale. Here the surface area is nearly double that of Piazza Armerina (6,340 sq. m), yet scholarly opinions, based on documentary evidence, allow a maximum of 12–15 years (E. Kitzinger, *The Mosaics of Monreale*, Palermo 1960, 24), and perhaps as little as 5–6 years (O. Demus, *The Mosaics of Norman Sicily*, London 1949, 145), for completion of the entire project.

19. See further Wilson 1982, 424–5.

20. Dunbabin 1978, 46–64 for a discussion of African hunting mosaics, including these two, and full bibliography.

21. ibid. 55 with pl. 29 and bibliography.

22. ibid. 56 with pl. 31 and bibliography.

23. Carandini 1967, 107.

24. Dunbabin 1978, 53–5 and pl. 24–8.

25. Mahjoubi 1967, 276.

26. See discussion in Salomonson 1965, 32–48 (*c.* AD 300).

27. ibid. 28, cf. 36. The animal scenes are in the corridor immediately outside the room with the hunting children mosaic.

28. ibid. 47; for some other African examples of this theme, Dunbabin 1978, 129, note 79.

29. Cf. also the great marine scene at Carthage, where the two are also found together, along with porticoed villas along the edges (Dunbabin 1978, 254 for bibliography – Carthage 45 – and pl. 126–7).

30. Again, even if Dorigo 1971, 132 and 166, is right to distinguish the Master of the Animal Heads as a separate designer, the identical type of laurel wreaths which surround each head is also used in rooms 4 (chapel), 28 (kissing couple) and 29 (fruit); this surely suggests that all four were the product of the same workshop, even if the designers were different (Dorigo assigns the last two floors to the Court Master). On the laurel wreath with the spikes and sashes, L'Orange 1965, 72–4.

31. Both from the Maison des Protomés at Thuburbo Maius (= Dunbabin 1978, 274, Thuburbo 4a-b); for photographs, L'Orange 1965, pl. IVc, VIIId and Yacoub 1970, fig. 96.

32. Dunbabin 1978, 91–2.

33. *Pace* Dorigo 1971, 142–4, who ascribes the Circus mosaic to the same designer as the Hunt mosaics, which I think unlikely.

34. Dunbabin 1978, 90–1.

35. Carandini 1964, 51–2; Carandini 1967, 106–7, supported by Dunbabin 1978, 201.

36. Kähler 1969, 45; and see note 39 of ch. 1.

37. The fact that the steps partly cut into the corridor floor, which has been repaired, need only imply a rebuilding of the steps, not that the whole *triconchos* is later (as Lugli 1963, 61 believed).

38. See note 41 of ch. 1.

39. They share the feature of what Dorigo calls (1971, 139) 'inlaid framing, variously tinted, in which the significance of the organic bodily build is altogether missing'. Cf. also the comments of Dunbabin 1978, 200 note 16.

40. The idea of Gentili 1952a, 46 note 41, that these signs spelt a name ending in . . . *chos* (? the mosaicist's signature), is ludicrous.

41. E.g. at Carthage (Salomonson 1965, 22–3 and pl. X.2), Sousse (ibid. IX.3; no. 14 in Dunbabin 1978, 270, '?Beginning of 4th century'), Nabeul (dated post 316/7, Darmon 1980). There also seems to be one on the forehead of the seated figure at the centre of the Tellaro hunting mosaic (pl. 49), which may possibly be an indication that this is a later creation of the same North African workshop which laid the Piazza Armerina floors.

Chapter 3

1. The structures still partly visible immediately north of the apse of the large hall (30) – see plate 23 – would appear to be so, as one of the rooms partly overlies the water channel of the adjacent aqueduct which has been destroyed at

this point. The structures farther north lie under a great blanket of soil, part of the earth slip which has preserved the walls of the villa itself to such a great height; there are therefore no surface sherds. Another large area, however, extending for some 300 m west of the western aqueduct as far as the river (foreground of plate 2) is covered by surface sherds, but the presence of glazed wares and the absence of distinctive late-Roman pottery or roof tiles indicate that this is part of the Arab and Norman village which grew up at the site (p. 42).

2. The base of the mill lies in the angle between the perimeter wall of the entrance court (2) and the large latrine (6). Two intact *dolia*, now standing south-west of the *caldaria*, were apparently found 200 m east of the villa (information from Signor Anzaldi, head custodian), and other *dolia* fragments are piled up west of the great entrance (1). There is also a quernstone at present in the basin of 17A.

3. Antonine Itinerary 94.5. For the tile-stamp, Adamesteanu 1955, 210, and for the site in general Adamesteanu 1963 and Bonomi 1966.

4. San Cono: *Notizie degli Scavi* 1957, 204–5; Brajemi: *Fasti Archeologici* xviii-xix (1963–4), 7446–7.

5. Gentili 1969, especially 10 (Monte Navone), 22–7, 29–31, 101 (Montagna di Marzo).

6. Gentili 1950, 292–3; Hayes 1972, 199–200 (form 180).

7. Ampolo et al. 1971, 143–6.

8. Cf. MacMullen 1974, 38–9 with 159–60 (notes 33–4); and in general Jones 1964, 781–8.

9. Antonine Itinerary 95.7 and 88.3.

10. I owe this suggestion to Professor A. L. F. Rivet. For the name Philosophus, cf. *Inscriptiones Graecae* III, 1079 (from Attica, third century AD or later).

11. E.g. Li Gotti 1951; Pace 1955a, 45, n.40; Ragona 1962, 51–4; and Coarelli 1980, 385–6. No FIL SOF tile stamps are recorded from the villa at Piazza Armerina.

12. E.g. bath-buildings near Milazzo (prov. of Messina) and Acireale (Catania) and at Misterbianco (Catania); mosaics at S. Nicolo di Carini (Palermo), Cusumano near Mazara (Trapani) and near Halaesa (Messina). An account of these will be provided by me in a forthcoming book on Roman Sicily.

13. A large part of the villa at Castroreale San Biagio (Messina), however, was uncovered by Gentili, but its heyday was in the first and second centuries AD.

14. Voza 1972–3, 190–2; Voza 1973; Voza 1976–7, 572–4.

15. So Dunbabin 1978, 212. One wonders if Sicilian demand was sufficient to make it worthwhile for an African company to set up a branch workshop in a city such as Syracuse.

16. Sherds of African red slip pottery of Hayes forms 8B and 9A (Hayes 1972, 32–7) were picked up by myself on a visit to the site in 1973.

17. Personal observation. Agnello 1971 reports the earlier discoveries of two 'grape-presses' at this villa.

18. Voza 1976–7, 574–9; also his communication to the 5th International Congress of studies on Ancient Sicily, Palermo 1980, publication forthcoming in *Kokalos*.

19. Personal observation; from a room to the west of the peristyle.

20. Romanelli 1970, 252–8; Sarnowski 1978.

21. Origins of the *triconchos*: Lavin 1962, esp. 26. But it appears first in the east, in the second-century governor's palace at Bostra in Syria and probably also in the third-century residence of the *Dux Ripae* at Dura-Europos: see Boethius and Ward-Perkins 1970, 445 and 451–2.

22. Plan of Portus Magnus house: Boethius and Ward-Perkins 1970, 532. Semicircular court, cf. Bulla Regia in Tunisia: Beschaouch, Hanoune and Thébert 1977, 111 and figs 105 and 109. Interlocking tubular tiles: see chapter 1, note 16.

23. Boethius and Ward-Perkins 1970, 330, 531–2; Swoboda 1969, 5–28, 61–76.

24. Cf. especially Krencker and Krüger 1929, 187–235 and Stucchi 1957; for a similarly shaped *frigidarium* at Bulla Regia, Beschaouch, Hanoune and Thébert 1977, fig. 90. For Italian parallels, Lugli 1963, 50–1, 62–5 and 70–3.

25. Personal observation; for the baths there are preliminary notes in *Klearchos* 23–4 (1964), 106, 108; 25–8 (1965), 139, 141; 29–32 (1966), 225; and *Atti del V Convegno di Studi sulla Magna Graecia*, 1966, 225-6

26. Small 1980 with discussion on 95–6. For a list of known Roman villas in Calabria, see *Klearchos* 29–32 (1966), 41, note 13; and for a discussion of Roman villas in Basilicata, Small and Buck 1980.

27. Dunbabin 1978, 214–6, and Wilson 1982, 426. For the villa as a whole, Ghislanzoni 1962; more recent work is unpublished.

28. Berti 1976 for the most recent full account, with earlier bibliography; more briefly Duval 1978, 32–9.

29. See especially *Ep*. II. 2; and for its place in the social life of Sidonius, Stevens 1933, esp. 64–84, and Dill 1899, 160–78.

30. E.g. the ladies' dining-room (*triclinium matronale*), winter dining-room (*triclinium hiemale*), living room (*diaeta*), small dining-room (*cenatiuncula*), drawing room (*deversorium*), weaving room (*textrinum*), ante room (*consistorium*), storeroom (*cella pinaria*), a covered corridor (*cryptoporticus*), bedrooms (*cubicula*).

31. Fouet 1969.

32. Fouet 1978 and 1979, with earlier bibliography.

33. *Corpus Inscriptionum Latinarum* XIII.128. Some other wealthy late-Roman villas in Gaul, none as large as Montmaurin or Valentine, are included in the survey of Percival 1976, 67–82.

34. Gorges 1979, 403 with earlier bibliography. Milreu: ibid. 480–1. A *triconchos* also occurs in the villa at Ecija (ibid. 374–5 with pl. XLVI.1), while the large apsed room is a common feature in many late-Roman villas in Spain, such as Almenara de Adaja (ibid. 437–8) and Aguilafùente (ibid. 355). The nearest villas in the Iberian peninsula to approach Milreu in size are Liedena near Navarra, 170 m by 75 m (but the residential block is only 50 m sq.), Torre de Palma in Portugal (main block including farm buildings, is *c*. 110 m square) and Centcelles, where the only excavated wing is 100 m long (Gorges 1979, 323–4, 465–6 and 411–2).

35. Lysons 1797; Royal Commission on Historical Monuments 1976, 132–4, for a recent summary and re-assessment.

36. Modrijan 1971. The chronology of this villa is, however, rather uncertain. The first villa was laid out in the early second century AD, but the large hall (18 m × 9 m) and other rooms were added when the villa was reshaped, apparently at the end of the third century.

37. See in general Thomas 1964 and Mócsy 1974, 299–308.

38. Unless this site has more than purely agricultural significance and was a supplies centre for the striking force (*comitatenses*) of the late-Roman field army operating in this area. Fenékpuszta is described in Thomas 1964, 60–8; cf. also Percival 1976, 90 and 176.

39. The most accessible accounts are Srejović 1975 and Duval 1971, 115–22; Čanak-Medić 1978, the definitive report, is scarce outside Yugoslavia. (I am grateful to Prof. A. Mócsy for first supplying me with this reference, and to Dr J.

Sašel for sending me a copy of the monograph.) For earlier work here Mano-Zisi 1956 and Popović 1961.

40. The *orbiculi* (oval shoulder patches) on the cloaks at both villas are supposed to bear the same signs; but there is nothing special about such clothing in the late-Roman period: see in detail Rinaldi 1964–5, esp. 222–7, 248–9.

41. Mócsy 1974, 302 and pl. 43b; cf. also *Princeton Encyclopaedia of Classical Sites*, 605–6.

42. Not to be confused with the massive outer fortifications which still stand. These are believed by Mrs Čanak-Medić to be of fourth-century date, possibly Constantinian, and are quite distinct from the earlier walls of undoubted Diocletianic date, of which only the west gate and an interval tower have been excavated.

43. Some of the embellishments, however, seem not to have been completed until after his death in 311. Other helpful general discussions of late-Roman villas include Swoboda 1969, especially 133–67 and 281–91, and Cagiano de Azevedo 1966; Paribeni 1940 is more superficial and, despite its title, includes villas which no member of the *potentiores* will have been near. There seem to be no country mansions from the eastern half of the Roman Empire relevant to the discussion. Certain aspects of the large building (*c.* 120 m by 90 m) in the town of Nea Paphos (Cyprus), currently under excavation by a Polish team, have been compared to Piazza Armerina (central apsed room in middle of south wing, long room with rounded ends in the entrance complex of the east wing), but the main layout is now thought to be of early imperial date (*Bulletin de Correspondence Hellénique* ciii (1979), 715; fig 82 for plan).

44. L'Orange 1952, 1953, 1955, 1956, 1965, 1966; all except 1965 are reprinted in L'Orange 1973. There is a shortened version of the 1965 article in Picard and Stern 1965, 305–14, also reprinted in L'Orange 1973.

45. Gentili 1950, contrast 1956, 1959, 1966 etc.

46. Kähler 1961–2, 1969, 1973; Polzer 1973; Settis 1975; accepted also by Bovini 1970, 56.

47. L'Orange 1965, 84.

48. ibid. 95–6.

49. See especially L'Orange 1955.

50. L'Orange 1965, 100 (Hercules), cf. Gentili, *La Giara* iv (1955), 47.

51. *L'Année Epigraphique* 1956, 100: AED HV|GALLO restored as AED [es sacrae D(omini) N(ostri) M. Aur(eli) Val(eri) Maximiani]|H(erculei) V(ictoris) GALL[orum liberatoris?]; 'the sacred shrines of His Majesty M. Aurelius Valerius Maximian Herculeus, conqueror, freer of the Gauls'. For a comment on this and the possibility that two other fragments belong to the same inscription, see Pucci in Ampolo et al. 1971, 249–50. The last line has recently been reinterpreted as co]H V GALL [orum referring to a fifth cohort of Gauls (Manganaro, forthcoming).

52. It also occurs on the cuffs and borders of the tunic worn by the figure on the right of the statue of Diana in the Small Hunt; above the tree in the apse of room 34; in the pediment of the middle temple at the north end of the Circus mosaic; as the central emblem in the 'shrine' opening off the peristyle (4), and in two corners of each of the guilloche squares which contain the animal-head medallions (e.g. plate 4). For the 'Herculeius' interpretation, Gentili 1966, 13 and elsewhere in his writings. The claim that the letter H appears on the shoulder badge of the attendant on the right of the so-called *dominus* (plate 54), made by L'Orange (1952, 128, note 1) and accepted by Gentili (1959, 23) and Polzer (1973, 146), is totally illusory (as Pace 1955a, 112, pointed out).

53. Settis 1975, 923–87; Polzer 1973, 147–8 also stresses Maxentius' links with

Rome, allegedly stronger than Maximian's. The theory that the dominance of animals among the Piazza Armerina mosaics is symbolic of the emperor's triumph over the bestial and the barbarous was first expounded by L'Orange 1953.

54. Carandini 1964, 17; contrast L'Orange 1965, 81–7. For the fifth-century diptych, cf. (e.g.) D. E. Strong, *Roman Art* (London 1976), pl. 245. See also note 72 below.

55. As Settis, himself a proponent of imperial ownership, has pointed out: see especially his review of Kähler 1973 in *Gnomon* 1976, 400–4, esp. 403–4. The mushroom-shaped staffs in the hands of these officials have also been claimed as having 'imperial' significance (Gentili 1959, 70; L'Orange 1965, 87–8); but they appear too in representations of what are undoubtedly not emperors, such as on gold-leaf glass (Cagiano de Azevedo 1967–8, 132), as well as on the Tellaro mosaic (plate 49).

56. On the lack of imperial *dignitas* in these figures, Cagiano de Azevedo 1961, 17–19. It has also been pointed out (Di Vita 1972–3, 257; Marrou 1978, 256; Dunbabin 1978, 204–5) that the personage of the emperor was held in such reverence in the late Empire that the idea of an imperial portrait on a *floor*, where it could be trodden on, was unthinkable.

57. Manganaro 1959, 247–8; cf. Settis, *Gnomon* 1976, 403.

58. For the *hedera* and the amphitheatre *sodalitates* in Africa, Dunbabin 1978, 74–8. The later repair at the foot of the central steps from the Hunt corridor, including the panel mentioning Bonufatius and depicting millet stalks flowing from a kantharos, has also been connected with the amphitheatre *sodalitates* (Pucci in Ampolo et al. 1971, 250–1; Beschaouch 1977, 501–3). On the other hand the *hedera* is increasingly employed without amphitheatrical connotations as the fourth century progresses (Dunbabin 1978, 171). The occurrence of the *hedera* at Piazza Armerina has usually been interpreted as a lucky symbol (e.g. Toynbee 1975, 217), as a sign of victory in the games (Manganaro 1959, 247–8), or simply as an ornamental motif (Bovini 1970, 40–1).

59. Manganaro 1959; H. Bloch in Momigliano 1963, 193–217. Theories about the *triconchos* mosaics are briefly summarized and refuted by Dunbabin 1978, 203–4.

60. E.g. on the Mithraic tomb at Gargaresh, Tripoli: Romanelli 1970, pl. 264.

61. So Manganaro 1959, 248–9.

62. Pensabene in Ampolo et al. 1971, 207–19; cf. Kähler 1973, 20–5 and Gentili 1956. Lugli 1963, 36 and 42, also notes that some of the capitals, and some of the column shafts too, are of re-used marble.

63. E.g. at Ostia (*Scavi di Ostia* VI, Rome 1969, passim) and Kenchreae in Greece (*Kenchreai: Eastern Port of Corinth* II, Leiden 1976, passim). For Sidonius' 'columns of purple', *Ep.* II.2.8. On the porphyry design at Piazza Armerina, cf. Pensabene in Ampolo et al. 1971, 223–4. The use of small pieces of porphyry along with many other coloured stones in *opus sectile* work is a far cry from whole statues (as at Gamzigrad, p. 84) or sarcophagi carved in porphyry, which do normally carry imperial overtones at this period (R. Delbrück, *Antike Porphyrywerke*, Berlin 1932).

64. See the recent discussion by Pisani Sartorio and Calza 1976, esp. 124–5 and 148–54 with full references to earlier literature.

65. Nash 1961, 190 for bibliography. The internal dimensions of the hall, excluding narthex, are approximately 34 m by 14 m; cf. Piazza Armerina 30 m by 14 m; Ravenna, 27 m by 11 m; Mljet in Yugoslavia (on which see Duval 1971, 105–9 with bibliography) 31 m by 12 m. These compare very favourably with the size of audience halls in undoubted imperial ownership (e.g. Split 30 m by 14 m;

the Palatine 28 m by 20 m; contrast, however, Maxentius' villa on the via Appia, 38 m by 19 m, and the Basilica at Trier, 67 m by 27 m). For other examples of large halls on private property, see Pisani Sartorio and Calza 1976, 124 note 50.

66. Cf. Mazzarino 1953; Pace 1955a, 111–9.

67. Lactantius *De Mort. Pers.* 26; Zosimus II.10.12.

68. Constantine did own properties in the *territorium Catinense* (*Liber Pontificalis*, ed. Duchesne, I, 174, lines 5–6), but there is no evidence that Piazza Armerina was one of them.

69. Manganaro forthcoming, following a suggestion first made by him in *Kokalos* xviii-xix (1972–3), 262–3.

70. Pucci in Ampolo et al. 1971, 252 (see fig. 115) read it as]M PORTI[cus, a reading dismissed without reason by Manganaro. Only the lower half of the letters survives. On what little is known about the collection and transport of grain in the provinces, see Rickman 1980, esp. 92–3, 120–2, and 222–5.

71. It is usually assumed that the absence of heated rooms except in the baths implies that the villa was used only as a summer residence (Kähler 1969, 44) or as a 'hunting lodge' (Gentili 1959, 12); but adequate heating during the winter could probably have been provided by portable braziers.

72. We do know that some emperors spared no expense in presenting lavish animal shows (Toynbee 1973, 18–19 collects the evidence), and presumably they enlisted the help of their procurators (cf. *Corpus Inscriptionum Latinarum* VI.10208). For Manganaro (forthcoming), the so-called *dominus* is the proconsul of Africa supervising the capture of animals on that continent, and the central figure in the corridor is the Urban praetor at Rome receiving the animals into the city. An alternative view of the Great Hunt (Marrou 1978), that it represents a military exercise of the Roman army, is based on a conviction that the figures directing operations are all wearing military dress, and is allegedly supported by passages in the ancient sources (especially Julius Africanus, *Cestoi* I.14), which show that the Roman army did sometimes hunt animals as a military exercise. But while no doubt such exercises frequently took place at local level, it seems unlikely that the Roman army would have been involved in the rounding up of beasts on a global scale, especially when the principal sources of such beasts (including those shown on the Great Hunt) lay either beyond the frontiers, where there were normally no troops, or in provinces such as Africa where very few soldiers were stationed; there is, moreover, no hint from the rest of the mosaics at Piazza Armerina that the owner who commissioned them had any strong military connections. The huntsmen on the Great Hunt are armed with shields and spears out of self-protection in a dangerous job, not because they are soldiers. Marrou (1978, 268–71) also interprets the dress (the cloak or *chlamys*) as exclusively military; but the study of Rinaldi (1964–5, especially 218–27) has shown that from the late third century onwards this garment was worn by civilians as well. The strongest argument in favour of Marrou's thesis is the occurrence of the flat-topped beret: apart from the Tetrarchic monuments (pp. 87, 88–9), it appears on numerous fourth-century Christian sarcophagi with scenes of the arrest of Peter, always worn by the two soldiers who flank him; and in the few remaining instances where it occurs in Roman art in other media (e.g. ivory diptych – see note 54 above; fresco in the via Latina catacomb, Rome), it is also worn by soldiers: I know of no certain representation where it is worn by a civilian. It is possible, however, that the sarcophagus evidence gives a misleading impression, just as we should also believe that the *chlamys* was exclusively military if we had only the sarcophagi to rely on (the evidence for its civilian use comes from works of art in other media: Rinaldi 1964–5, 225). In

fact, as evidence for male headgear from fourth-century monuments and artefacts is slight (apart from Phrygian caps worn by mythological figures, and conventional helmets), I see no reason why a predominantly military headgear could not also have been affected by civilians.

73. Compare an edict of 369 in which governors were told of their duty to live in their official residences where they would be available to all, and not to seek 'pleasant retreats' elsewhere (*Codex Theodosianus* I.16.12).

74. Compare the situation in Britain, where it is usually thought that areas *without* substantial villa-buildings were imperial estates; Percival 1976, 132–3.

75. Jones 1964, 786 with note 38 on p. 251 of vol. III (p. 1321 of the two-volume reprint). On the life-style of the late-Roman senatorial aristocracy, see also Matthews 1975, 1–31 and, in general, Dill 1899, 97–186.

76. Ammianus XIV.6.19.

77. See the passages cited by Toynbee 1973, 345 note 7. Chariot-drivers were sought from Sicily: Symmachus *Ep.* VI.42.

78. No Sicilian senators are known before the end of the first century AD and only two governors of Sicily were certainly natives of the island (Alpinius Magnus and Julius Claudius Peristerius, both fourth or fifth century). One member of the Sicilian aristocracy who preferred a quiet life of writing and reflection to the rigours of a political career was Firmicus Maternus, author of *Matheseos* (AD 334/7) and then of *De Errore Profanarum Religionum* (343/8).

79. Jones 1964, 737–63 (and 525–9 on the huge expansion of the senatorial class in the fourth century to avoid the tax burdens which fell on the town-councillor class); cf. also Arnheim 1972, 152–4.

80. Cf. Agennius Urbicus, *de Controversiis agrorum*: 'many estates are much bigger than city territories: moreover private estates have a not inconsiderable artisan population and villages surrounding the villa like towns' (or 'defences': the reading is uncertain); cf. also note 83. See in general Arnheim 1972, 144–7 and Matthews 1975, 79–80 and 343.

81. Dio LII.42.6; Tacitus *Annals* XII.23.1.

82. *Codex Theodosianus* VII.13.20.

83. *Vita Melaniae* I, ch. 18–21 (*Analecta Bollandiana* viii (1889), 33–5). Of one estate it was written that 'it had sixty small farms, comprising 400 agricultural slaves' (ch. 18) and of another that 'it was bigger than a very city, having baths, many craftsmen, gold- and silversmiths and bronze workers, as well as two bishops . . .' (ch. 21).

84. One of the group was the historian Rufinus, who watched the burning of Reggio Calabria by the Visigoths in 410 from there (J. P. Migne, *Patrologia Graeca* XII. 583–6).

85. *Inscriptiones Graecae* XII. 283.

86. For the last the evidence is a postscript (*subscriptio*) to Livy book VII, and is dated by the title 'urban prefect for the third time', a post he held in 408. For the other two, Symmachus *Epistulae* IV.71 and II.44. For the family as a whole in the context of pagan Rome, Momigliano 1963, 193–217.

87. Pace 1955a, 42–3; Cagiano de Azevedo 1961, 1967–8.

88. Ragona 1962, 1966.

89. *Codex Theodosianus* VIII.5.12.

90. Gentili 1950, 315, fig. 16, on the basis of an inscription including the letters ANIC . . .; but the lettering of the inscription is clearly early imperial, as Pace 1951, 459, pointed out; he restored the word as Germ]ANIC[o (followed by Manganaro, forthcoming).

91. S. Mazzarino in *Doxa* 1951, 136; cf. Manganaro 1959, 241–3.

92. An interpretation stressed by Laurenzi 1962, 312–3, Toynbee 1973, 27–8, and others; this seems more straightforward and logical than the involved symbolism conjectured by L'Orange and Settis.

93. Except, of course, for the griffin (see below), and possibly also for the 'heroic' encounters between hunters and felines, a stock motif, unless the latter are intended as an allusion to the amphitheatre *venationes*, the intended final destination of the animals. (The griffin, a symbol of Nemesis, is depicted seizing a cage in which a man is trapped; the message of the scene is probably that while man may hunt and kill animals now Nemesis in the form of death awaits him in the end; so Carandini 1971, 132, but for other interpretations, Toynbee 1973, 29, Settis Frugoni 1975, 27, and Dunbabin 1978, 203, note 33). Dunbabin 1978, 53–5, stresses the element of fantasy in the Great Hunt at Piazza Armerina; yet the scenes of capture and transportation of these beasts (as opposed to hunting and killing) bear every appearance of realism and are in fact rare in mosaic art: Tellaro in Sicily and Carthage (Dermech) and Hippo Regius in North Africa are instances. Could not the owners of all three properties have been directly involved in this industry, which 'must have been organized on an enormous scale and cost enormous sums' (Toynbee 1973, 20)? On Tellaro, cf. Toynbee 1975, 217.

94. On this point, Dunbabin 1978, 24.

95. Most obviously the Nicomachi Flaviani (p. 96). Cracco Ruggini 1980, 514 suggests the owner was 'a personage like L. Aradius Valerius Proculus', who was governor of Sicily (*c.* 325/8), later proconsul of Africa and twice prefect of Rome; he was of noble family and a pagan. This suggestion is developed more fully by Carandini in his forthcoming book on Piazza Armerina, but apart from Proculus' Sicilian governorship we have no evidence that either he or his family had interests in Sicily. For the strong suspicion that governorships were arranged in the late Empire so that public and private interests could coincide, see Matthews 1975, 23 and 25–31.

Bibliography

Adamesteanu, D. 1955. Due problemi topografici del retroterra gelese, *Rendiconti Accademia Lincei* x, 199–210.

Adamesteanu, D. 1963. Nuovi documenti paleocristiani nella Sicilia centro-meridionale, *Bollettino d'Arte* xlviii, 259–74.

Agnello, S. L. 1965. La villa romana di Piazza Armerina ai primi dell' 800, *Archivio Storico Siracusano* xi, 57–77.

Agnello, S. L. 1971. La villa romana di contrada Caddeddi: appunto bibliografico, *Archivio Storico Siracusano* n.s. i, 145–7.

Ampolo et al. 1971. Ampolo, C., Carandini, A., Pucci, G., Pensabene, P. La villa del Casale a Piazza Armerina. Problemi, saggi stratigrafici ed altre ricerche. *Mélanges de l'École Française de Rome, Antiquité* lxxxiii, 141–281.

Arnheim, M. W. T. 1972. *Senatorial Aristocracy in the Later Roman Empire* (Oxford).

Barreca, V., Sicari, G., and Cremona, F. 1967. Deformazione muscolare e stilizzazione delle figure nei mosaici della villa romana di Piazza Armerina, *Rivista di Anatomia Artistica* i, 31–44.

Bernabò Brea, L. 1947. Restauri dei mosaici romani del Casale, *Notizie degli Scavi* 1947, 250–3.

Berti, F. 1976. *Mosaici antichi in Italia, regione ottava: Ravenna* (Rome).

Beschaouch, A. 1977. Nouvelles recherches sur les sodalités de l'Afrique romaine, *Comptes rendus de l'Académie des Inscriptions et Belles-Lettres* 1977, 486–503.

Beschaouch, A., Hanoune, R. and Thébert, Y. 1977. *Les Ruines de Bulla Regia* (Rome).

Boethius, A., and Ward-Perkins, J. B. 1970. *Etruscan and Roman Architecture* (Harmondsworth).

Bonomi, L. 1966. Cimiteri paleocristiani di Sofiana, *Rivista di archeologia cristiana* xl, 169–220.

Bovini, G. 1970. I mosaici della villa romana di Piazza Armerina, *XVII Corso di Cultura sull'arte ravennate e bizantina* (Ravenna), 35–59.

Cagiano de Azevedo, M. 1961. I proprietari della villa di Piazza Armerina, in *Scritti di Storia dell'Arte in onore di Mario Salmi* I (Rome), 15–27.

Cagiano de Azevedo, M. 1966. Ville rustiche tardoantiche e installazioni agricole altomedievali, *Settimane di Studio del Centro Italiano di Studi sull'alto medioevo* (Spoleto) XIII, 662–94.

Cagiano de Azevedo, M. 1967–8. Questioni vecchie e nuove su Piazza

Armerina, *Rendiconti della Pontificia accademia romana di archeologia* xl, 123–50.

Čanak-Medić, M. 1978. *Kasnoantička Palata: Arkhitektura i Prostorni Sklop,* Saopshten'a XI. Republičkog Zavoda za Zashtitu Spomenika Kulture SR Srbije (Belgrade), with French summary.

Carandini, A. 1964. Ricerche sullo stile e la cronologia dei mosaici della villa di Piazza Armerina, *Studi Miscellanei* 7 (Rome) for 1961–2 (publ. 1964).

Carandini, A. 1967. La villa di Piazza Armerina, la circolazione della cultura figurativa africana nel tardo impero ed altre precisazioni, *Dialoghi di Archeologia* i, 93–120.

Carandini, A. 1971. Appunti sulla composizione del mosaico detto 'grande caccia' della villa del Casale a Piazza Armerina, *Dialoghi di Archeologia* iv-v, 120–34.

Coarelli, F. 1980. La cultura figurativa in Sicilia dalla conquista romana a Bisanzio, in Gabba and Vallet 1980, 373–92.

Cracco Ruggini, L. 1980. La Sicilia e la fine del mondo antico, in Gabba and Vallet 1980, 481–524.

Cultrera, G. 1940. Notiziario di scavi, scoperte, studi relativi all' impero romano, *Bullettino del Museo dell' Impero Romano* xi (appendix to *Bullettino Communale di Roma* lxviii), 129–30.

Daltrop, G. 1969. *Die Jagdmosaiken des römischen Villa bei Piazza Armerina* (Berlin).

Darmon, J-P. 1980. *Nympharum Domus. Les pavements de la maison des Nymphes à Neapolis (Nabeul, Tunisie) et leur lecture* (Leiden).

Dill, S. 1899. *Roman Society in the Last Century of the Western Empire*, 2nd ed. (London).

Di Vita, A. 1972–3. La villa di Piazza Armerina e l'arte musiva in Sicilia, *Kokalos* xviii-xix, 251–61.

Dorigo, W. 1971. *Late Roman Painting* (London).

Dunbabin, K. M. D. 1978. *The Mosaics of Roman North Africa* (Oxford).

Duval, N. 1971. Palais et forteresses en Yugoslavie: recherches nouvelles, *Bulletin de la Societé Nationale des Antiquaires de France* 1971, 99–128.

Duval, N. 1978. Comment reconnaître un palais imperial ou royale? Ravenne et Piazza Armerina, *Felix Ravenna* cxv, 27–62.

Fouet, G. 1969. *La villa gallo-romaine de Montmaurin*, XXth supplement to *Gallia* (Paris).

Fouet, G. 1978. La villa gallo-romaine de Valentine (Haute-Garonne). Aperçu préliminaire, *Revue de Comminges* xci, 145–57.

Fouet, G. 1979. Sauvetage d'une mosaique dans la villa de Valentine, *Revue de Comminges* xcii, 3–13.

Gabba, E. and Vallet G. (ed.) 1980. *La Sicilia antica* II (Naples).

Gentili, G. V. 1950. Grandiosa villa romana in contrada Casale, *Notizie degli scavi* 1950, 291–335.

Gentili, G. V. 1952a. I mosaici della villa romana del Casale di Piazza Armerina, *Bollettino d'Arte* xxxvii, 33–46.

Gentili, G. V. 1952b. La villa romana del Casale di Piazza Armerina, *Atti del I° Congresso Nazionale di Archeologia Cristiana* (Rome), 171–82.

Gentili, G. V. 1952c. Lucerne cristiano-bizantine e croce normanna nella villa imperiale di Piazza Armerina, *Nuovo Didaskaleion* v, 82–9.

Gentili, G. V. 1956. La villa imperiale di Piazza Armerina, *Atti del VII° Congresso di Storia dell' Architettura* (Palermo), 247–50.

Gentili, G. V. 1957. Le Gare del Circo nel mosaico di Piazza Armerina, *Bollettino d'Arte* xlii, 7–27.

Gentili, G. V. 1958. Architettura e mosaici della villa romana di Piazza Armerina, *Acta Congressus Madvigani I* (Copenhagen), 397–412.

Gentili, G. V. 1959. *La villa Erculia di Piazza Armerina, I mosaici figurati* (Rome).

Gentili, G. V. 1962. *Musaici di Piazza Armerina. Le scene di caccia* (Milan).

Gentili, G. V. 1966. *The Imperial Villa of Piazza Armerina* (Guidebooks to the Museums, Galleries and Monuments of Italy, no. 87), 3rd English edition (Rome).

Gentili, G. V. 1969. Piazza Armerina (Enna). Le anonime città di Montagna di Marzo e di Monte Navone, *Notizie degli Scavi* 1969, 2nd supplement.

Gentili, G. V. 1975–6. Il mosaico della 'lampadedromia' nella villa di Piazza Armerina, *Musei Ferraresi, Bollettino Annuale* v-vi, 194–202.

Ghislanzoni, E. 1962. *La villa romana in Desenzano* (Milan).

Gnoli, R. 1971. *Marmora Romana* (Rome).

Gorges, J-G. 1979. *Les Villas Hispano-romaines. Inventaire et Problématique archéologiques* (Paris).

Hayes, J. W. 1972. *Late Roman Pottery* (London).

Hervel, R. 1970. De Piazza Armerina à Lillebonne. Mosaistes et chasseurs, *Précis analytique des traveaux de l'Académie des Sciences, belles lettres et arts de Rouen 1969*, 113–23.

Jones, A. H. M. 1964. *The Later Roman Empire* (Oxford).

Kähler, H. 1961–2. Split and Piazza Armerina: residences of two emperor-tetrarchs, *Urbs* 1961–2, 97–109.

Kähler, H. 1969. La villa di Massenzio a Piazza Armerina, *Acta ad Archaeologiam et Artium Historiam Pertinentia* iv, 41–9.

Kähler, H. 1973. *Die Villa des Maxentius bei Piazza Armerina* (Monumenta artis romanae XII) (Berlin).

Krencker, D. and Krüger, E. 1929. *Die Trierer Kaiserthermen* (Augsburg).

Laurenzi, L. 1962. Il palazzo di Piazza Armerina: i suoi mosaici e l'arte di tardo-antico, *IX Corso di Cultura sull'arte ravennate e bizantina* (Ravenna), 307–13.

Lavin, I. 1962. The House of the Lord: aspects of the role of palace *triclinia* in the architecture of late antiquity and in the early Middle Ages, *Art Bulletin* xliv, 1–27.

Lavin, I. 1963. The hunting mosaics of Antioch and their sources. A study of compositional principles in the development of early medieval style, *Dumbarton Oaks Papers* xvii, 179–286.

Leanti, A. 1761. *Lo stato presente della Sicilia* (Palermo).

Li Gotti, A. 1951. Topografia antica del 'Casale' presso Piazza Armerina, *Archivio Storico per la Sicilia Orientale* xlvii, 150–60 (also reprinted separately, Caltagirone 1964).

L'Orange, H. P. 1952. È un palazzo di Massimiano Erculeo che gli scavi di Piazza Armerina portano alla luce?, *Symbolae Osloenses* xxix, 114–28.

L'Orange, H. P. 1953. Aquileia e Piazza Armerina. Un tema eroica ed un tema pastorale nell'arte religiosa della tetrarchia, *Studi Aquileiesi offerti a Giovanni Brusin* (Aquileia), 185–95.

L'Orange, H. P. 1955. The Adventus ceremony and the slaying of Pentheus represented on two mosaics c. 300, *Late Classical and Medieval Studies in honour of A. M. Friend Jr.* (Princeton), 7–14.

L'Orange, H. P. 1956. Il palazzo di Massimiano Erculeo di Piazza Armerina, *Studi in onore di Aristide Calderini e Roberto Paribeni* III (Milan), 593–600.

L'Orange, H. P. 1965. Nuovo contributo allo studio del Palazzo Erculio di Piazza Armerina, *Acta ad Archaeologiam et Artium Historiam Pertinentia* ii, 65–104.

L'Orange, H. P. 1966. Un sacrificio imperiale nei mosaici di Piazza Armerina, *Scritti in onore di E. Arslan* (Milan), 101–4.

L'Orange, H. P. 1973. *Likeness and Icon. Selected Studies in Classical and Early Mediaeval Art* (Odense).

Lugli, G. 1963. Contributo alla storia edilizia della villa romana di Piazza Armerina, *Rivista dell' Istituto Nazionale di Archeologia e Storia dell' Arte* xi-xii, 28–82.

Lysons, S. 1797. *An account of Roman Antiquities discovered at Woodchester in the County of Gloucester* (London).

MacMullen, R. 1974. *Roman Social Relations 50 BC–AD 284* (Yale).

Mahjoubi, M. A. 1967. Découverte d'une nouvelle mosaique de chasse à Carthage, *Comptes rendus de l'Académie des Inscriptions et Belles-Lettres* 1967, 264–77.

Manganaro, G. 1959. Aspetti pagani dei mosaici di Piazza Armerina, *Archeologia Classica* xi, 241–50.

Manganaro, G. forthcoming. Die Villa von Piazza Armerina, Residenz des kaiserlichen Prokurators, und ein an sie gebundenes Emporium von Enna, paper delivered at Humboldt Institute, Berlin, 1979.

Mano Zisi, D. 1956. Le castrum de Gamzigrad et ses mosaiques, *Archaeologia Iugoslavica* ii, 67–84.

Marrou, H.-I. 1978. Sur deux mosaiques de la villa romaine de Piazza Armerina, in H.-I. Marrou, *Christiana Tempora. Mélanges d'histoire, d'archéologie, d'épigraphie et de patristique.* Collections, École française de Rome 35 (Paris), 253–95.

Matthews, J. 1975. *Senatorial Aristocracy and Imperial Court AD 364–425* (Oxford).

Mazzarino, S. 1953. Sull'otium di Massimiano Erculio dopo la abdicazione, *Rendiconti Accademia dei Lincei* viii, 417–21.

Mócsy, A. 1974. *Pannonia and Upper Moesia* (London).

Modrijan, W. 1971. *Der römische Landsitz von Löffelbach* (Graz).

Momigliano, A. (ed.) 1963. *Conflict between Paganism and Christianity in the Fourth Century* (Oxford).

Nash, E. 1961 and 1962. *Pictorial Dictionary of Ancient Rome*, two volumes: I (1961) and II (1962) (London).

Neuerburg, N. 1959. Some considerations on the architecture of the Imperial Villa at Piazza Armerina, *Marsyas* viii, 22–9.

Orsi, P. 1931. Notiziario di scavi, scoperte, studi relativi all' impero romano, *Bullettino del Museo dell' Impero Romano* ii (appendix to *Bullettino Communale di Roma* lix), 99–100.

Pace, B. 1951. Note su una villa romana presso Piazza Armerina, *Rendiconti Accademia dei Lincei* vi, 454–76.

Pace, B. 1955a. *I mosaici di Piazza Armerina* (Rome).

Pace, B. 1955b. Theatralia 2. Coreografie in Acqua, in *Anthemon. Studi in onore di Carlo Anti* (Florence), 312–7.

Paribeni, R. 1940. Le dimore dei *potentiores* nel basso impero, *Mitteilungen des deutschen archäologischen Instituts, Römische Abteilung* lv, 131–48.

Percival, J. 1976. *The Roman Villa. An Historical Introduction* (London).

Picard, G. C. 1978. Les romains en côte d'Ivoire, *Archéologia* no. 116, 22–7.

Picard, M. G. and Stern, H. 1965 (ed.) *La Mosaique Gréco-Romaine* (Paris).

Pisani Sartorio, G. and Calza, R. 1976. *La villa di Massenzio sulla via Appia* (Rome).

Polzer, J. 1973. The villa at Piazza Armerina and the numismatic evidence, *American Journal of Archaeology* lxxvii, 139–50.

Popović, V. 1961. Antički Gamzigrad, *Limes u Jugoslaviji* i, 145–53.

Ragona, A. 1962. *Il proprietario della villa romana di Piazza Armerina* (Caltagirone).

Ragona, A. 1966. *L'obelisco di Constanzo II e la datazione dei mosaici di Piazza Armerina* (Caltagirone).

Renard, M. 1960. Ulysse et Polyphème: à propos d'une mosaique de Piazza Armerina, *Hommages à Leon Herrmann* (Brussels), 655–68.

Rickman, G. 1980. *The Corn Supply of Ancient Rome* (Oxford).

Rinaldi, M. L. 1964–5. Il costume romano e i mosaici di Piazza Armerina, *Rivista dell' Istituto Nazionale di Archeologia e Storia dell' Arte* xiii-xiv, 200–68.

Romanelli, P. 1970. *Topografia e archeologia dell' Africa romana* (Turin).

Royal Commission on Historical Monuments, 1976. *Ancient and Historical Monuments in the County of Gloucester. Volume One. Iron Age and Romano-British Monuments in the Gloucestershire Cotswolds* (London).

Salomonson, J. W. 1965. *La mosaique aux chevaux de l'Antiquarium de Carthage* (The Hague).

Sarnowski, T. 1978. *Les representations de villas sur les mosaiques africaines tardives* (Wroclaw).

Sear, F. B. 1970. The late Roman villa at Piazza Armerina, in W. A. Alvarez and K. H. A. Gohrbrant (ed.), *Geology and History of Sicily* (Tripoli).

Settis, S. 1975. Per l'interpretazione di Piazza Armerina, *Mélanges de l'École Française de Rome, Antiquité* lxxxvii, 873–994.

Settis Frugoni, C. 1975. Il grifone e la tigre nella 'grande caccia' di Piazza Armerina, *Cahiers Archéologiques* xxiv, 21–32.

Small, A. M. 1980. S. Giovanni di Ruoti: some problems in the interpretation of the structures, *Roman Villas in Italy: Recent excavations and research* (ed. K. Painter), British Museum Occasional Paper No. 24 (London), 91–109.

Small, A. M. and Buck, R. J. 1980. The topography of Roman villas in Basilicata, *Studi in onore D. Adamesteanu. Attività archeologica in Basilicata 1964–77* (Matera), 561–70.

Srejović, J. 1975. An imperial Roman palace in Serbia, *Illustrated London News* (Archaeology 2909), October 1975, 97–9.

Stevens, C. E. 1933. *Sidonius Apollinaris and his age* (Oxford).

Stucchi, S. 1957. Le piante delle terme romane d'Africa ed i loro rapporti con quelle di Roma e dell' Europa, *Atti del V° Convegno Nazionale di Storia dell' Architettura*, Perugia 1948 (Florence).

Swoboda, K. M. 1969. *Römische und romanische Paläste*, 3rd edition (Graz).

Thomas, E. B. 1964. *Römische Villen in Pannonien* (Budapest).

Toynbee, J. M. C. 1973. *Animals in Roman Life and Art* (London).

Toynbee, J. M. C. 1975. Review of Kähler 1973 in *Journal of Roman Studies* xlv, 216–7.

Traversari, G. 1960. *Gli spettacoli in acqua nel teatro tardo antico* (Rome).

van den Broek, R. 1972. *The Myth of the Phoenix* (Leiden).

Voza, G. 1972–3. Intervento: Attività della Soprintendenza alle antichità per la Sicilia orientale, *Kokalos* xviii-xix, 186–92.

Voza, G. 1973. Mosaici della 'Villa del Tellaro', in *Archeologia nella Sicilia sud-orientale* (ed. P. Pelagatti and G. Voza) (Naples), 175–9.

Voza, G. 1976–7. L'attività della Soprintendenza alle antichità della Sicilia orientale. Parte II, *Kokalos* xxii-xxiii, 551–85.

Wilson, R. J. A. 1979. Brick and tiles in Roman Sicily, *Roman Brick and Tile* (ed. A. McWhirr), British Archaeological Reports Supplementary Series 68 (Oxford), 11–43.

Wilson, R. J. A. 1982. Roman mosaics in Sicily: the African connection, *American Journal of Archaeology* lxxxvi, 413–28.

Yacoub, M. 1970. *Le Musée du Bardo. Musée antique* (Tunis).

Index

Numbers in brackets are room numbers (see plate 1); numbers in italics refer to the plates. The notes have only been indexed where substantial additional material is discussed.